IT'S NEVER

BEYOND THE END

ALEX B. RACO

IT'S NEVER THE END

PAST LIVES PRESENT DESTINY

Regression therapy following the teachings of Dr. Brian Weiss

First edition: May 2016

Copyright © 2015 Alex B. Raco
All rights reserved.
Including the right of reproduction in whole or in part in any form.
www.terapiaregresiva.org

Cover design: Giorgio Gandolfo
Editing: Donica Raco Sapiano and Nathaniel Edwards

ISBN: 1530643996
ISBN-13: 978-1530643998

All of the characters, situations and places cited in this book are real. Names have been changed to protect individual privacy.

The author of this book does not dispense medical advice or prescribe the use of any technique as a form of treatment for physical, emotional or medical problems without the advice of a physician, either directly or indirectly. The intent of the author is only to offer information of a general nature to help you in your quest for emotional and spiritual well-being. In the event you use any of the information in this book for yourself, which is your constitutional right, the author and the publisher assume no responsibility for your actions.

*To Elena,
without whom this book would not exist*

CONTENTS

The end and the beginning	1
Alex or Sophie?	19
Hypnosis and myths	47
Problems and memories	71
Consciousness and the brain	95
Parents and children	119
Animals and souls	141
Soul mates	157

THE END AND THE BEGINNING

"I wake up suddenly to a loud and abrupt noise in the distance. I think it's thunder. I feel like I must have been sleeping for months. My body is numb and rigid, my head is heavy. I try to open my eyes but the light is too agonizing. I'm lying down on something hard and humid, something that I don't recognize. Strangely, this doesn't bother me. It's as if my body has taken to its new form. But where am I?

I try to open my eyes again. I stretch my arms out in front of my face to protect them from the light. I discover that my arms are covered by a thick layer of dark hair. They're massive, muscular, stocky arms. Instead of hands, I have big brown nails encrusted with earth. Claws. I'm... I'm... I'm a bear!

I'm a big and strong bear. I'm not in my room but in a cave, in the middle of a thick, immense forest."

I can imagine the shocked look on your face, dear reader. It is probably the same look that I had when I listened to this story, seated in the armchair of my office in Barcelona one warm April morning a few years back. The words came out, almost automatically, from the mouth of a thin blonde girl not even 30 years of age, whom I would have described as shy when she entered into my office for the first time.

The young woman, who I will call Marta to protect her identity, came from Italy to see me. The previous year she had gone to a past life regression seminar. She told me that she found my personal story particularly touching, as Dr. Brian Weiss had invited me onto the stage in front of more than a thousand people to tell it. She traveled more than a thousand miles to come to Barcelona, where I've dedicated myself for years to past life regression therapy, following the teachings of Dr. Weiss. With over 600 regressions behind me, this was the first time I had ever witnessed a person seeing his or her past life through the eyes of a bear.

For those unfamiliar with this topic, let me briefly describe what past life regression therapy consists of. It begins when I induce the person into a moderate hypnotic state that stimulates the activation of certain cerebral areas. I would describe it as a state of hyper-conscience during which the subject is able to access seemingly forgotten memories. I will explain the activated areas and their functions in detail, as well as debunk many myths on hypnosis, in a following chapter.

Listening to Marta's words, the possibility came to me that she might be making all of this up. I thought that maybe I hadn't put her into a deep enough hypnotic state. However, all of the circumstances suggested otherwise: Marta was completely immobile, lying down on the chaise longue in the dim light of my office; I could clearly see her eyes moving rapidly and recognize that they were in a state of REM (Rapid Eye Movement).

Behind her closed eyelids, her breathing was deep and regular and tears were dripping down her cheeks. All the signs of a deep hypnotic state, I thought. In that moment, that complicated and at times uncomfortable machine that resides in all of our craniums made me remember a few animal ethology studies I had undertaken in my youth.

"What colors are the plants in the forest?" I asked her immediately.

"I don't know," said Marta. "I can't really distinguish the colors. It is all brown, different shades of similar colors at the bark of the trees. It's as if I were seeing everything through a photographic filter." My heart started beating frantically.

As a young man I got the chance to study animal behavior in a course in New York. Everything I had learned perfectly confirmed Marta's words. Animals don't see colors like we do, but in a form very similar to what the girl had just described.

"Do you live there? In that cave?" I asked her.

"Yes. But the whole forest is mine. It's all mine." she said without a moment of hesitation.

"Everything that I see is mine. I am the master of the forest." she added.

"What sensations are you feeling?" I continued.

"It's chilly here and I'm fat and heavy."

"Where are your parents?" I asked her.

"I don't know," she replied, after thinking about it for a couple of seconds. "I don't remember anything. I don't have memories. I can't even remember my parents. I don't remember anything about what happened before now."

My level of excitement was increasing. And by now it was obvious that Marta was not imagining anything. The cerebral memory functions work very differently in animals. And bears are solitary animals; their only moments of socialization with their own species are the times a mother spends with her children or the brief period in which males and females come together to reproduce.

Marta's story that she was a bear in one of her past lives astonished me immensely. I've witnessed many incredible experiences but it was the first time that something like this had happened to me. I know why I was so surprised. Until then I had witnessed every type of experience and life, told by people in a state of trance: soldiers, Roman maids, Mongolian warriors, farmers, but this was the first time that someone had claimed to be an animal. Only after having spoken with Emanuela; a dear friend from Rome also certified by Dr. Weiss with whom I did my first regressions, did I confirm that lives in animal form, while rare, can occur in people who were American Indians in past lives. I'm referring to animal totems, spiritual guides that American Indians met with techniques similar to those of meditation or hypnosis today. I also draw inspiration from the work of Carl Jung, the psychologist and father of analytical psychology, who deals with the relationship between animals and the human psyche.

Marta's case was certainly unique and surprising; and yet still today, after hundreds of regressions, I continue to be astonished at what I saw.

The ability to become accustomed to 'the incredible' depends on the brain, a strange organ that belongs to our earthly dimension and pretends to have control over everything, including things that even it cannot understand.

By now I should have it mastered. Even if up until a few years ago, I myself would not have believed anything I'm about to tell you. And if someone had talked to me about past lives, I would have laughed in their face. I guess my ideas have changed.

It all started during Christmas vacation 2007, when after a brief trip to Rome to visit my family of origin, I decided to spend a few days in Milan, where I lived for 14 years. At that time, I was still a manager of one of the many multinationals where I had the fortune, or misfortune, of working. I started young; at 25 years old I already had a Bachelor's degree and an MBA from Bocconi University in Milan as well as my first job at a semi-managerial level. By now, after 14 years, I had a career that had taken me from one company to another, allowing me to start my own ventures and to live in various European cities. That Christmas I was really hoping to meet with many of my old friends that I hadn't had any way to see regularly after my move to Barcelona. Particularly, I was hoping to see my dear friend Patrizia, a veterinarian of about my age that I've known for more than 20 years. Her mother passed away in July of that same year. She was an adorable woman named Lia, who showered me with compliments every time we met, expressing her affection towards me. I knew how much Patrizia, an only child in a love-hate relationship, relied on her mother. I knew how much she felt her absence. This is why I decided to pass by her clinic to say hello.

It's always fun going to see her at work. While I was waiting with a woman who was describing to me the vicissitudes of her poor sick cat (who was looking at us miserably from his portable crate), the memories of a time years before came to mind, the time when I brought Patrizia my cat. I remembered her words to me after I described the emptiness I felt when Brenda died (that was my cat's name).

"I believe it. In the last ten years you've changed everything. You've changed cities, houses, jobs, you've even changed partners. The only constant in your life has been this cat." Truer words have never been spoken.

Today, with what I have had the pleasure of learning about the course of the soul, I'd like to think that our beloved companion animals are meant to accompany us during moments of our lives. They act as small messengers, celestial masters of the infinite, unconditional love of which we are all made. As witnessed by the American Indians, animals are real souls or emanations of our spiritual guides. In every precious moment, they help with our daily existence, in which love reminds us of the divine essence of any natural being. In the meantime, Patrizia was finishing up the woman's cat appointment. It was finally time to see her again.

"Come to our place for dinner," she said, in a peremptory tone that did not require an answer. Patrizia is the sweetest and most respectful person in the world, but at the same time, as a Taurus, she is stubborn and resolute. It was therefore useless to stall. I accepted her invitation with pleasure.

I drove with her until we reached a small city just outside Milan where she lives with her boyfriend. We immersed ourselves into the geometrically perfect streets of the residential complex, in which all of the similar and luxurious homes reminded me of an American television series. She began to tell me about how devastated she was after her mother's death. The binding of her existence seemed to be coming apart and she was living a moment of existential crisis. We entered the circular plaza adjacent to her small villa, identical to the other four or five facing us.

Mia, a Chihuahua she adopted after it was left behind by the unfortunate passing of a friend, came wagging her tail as we opened the gate. Patrizia had always adopted her cats and dogs, never bred. She'd always tried to help any defenseless animal. I remember when she kept and cared for a street pigeon for weeks that had been freed by a clinic. She even gave him a name, Gerry. Her compassion towards the animal world was unquantifiable and many times the price she paid was, well…not being paid. And I criticized her for this. In the obtuse and materialistic vision of life that I believed in up until a few years ago, there was no room for volunteering. I appreciated that she was doing good but I judged her because she was not getting paid. It's incredible how one can change. Still today, at 49 years of age, I fail to recognize the person that I was and the miracle that could come out of a single, fortuitous, episode—like the one that was about to happen. Marco, Patrizia's boyfriend, and all the other happy canines came to welcome us as we entered the house. Marco, a business executive, had just returned home from work and was preparing dinner. Patrizia entered the house like an earthquake and in a charitable way she scolded him for not having set the table. She then moved to prepare the dog food. The dogs are the main priority in the domestic economy of Patrizia's life, and they have always been. We mere guests can wait. We're human and we can understand. Marco hugged me and asked all kinds of questions about my new life in Barcelona, about how work was going and about how I was physically.

Around ten years ago I started to experience symptoms similar to those of Crohn's disease, a chronic autoimmune disease that can affect various zones of the gastrointestinal tract. It all began during a lunch break when I worked as a manager of the creative department of Walt Disney in Milan. I had gone to eat with some colleagues and I remember perfectly, even today, the large salad with raw artichokes that I ordered. For the next two days I was unable to eat anything at all. I was at the mercy of my abdominal pain and my stomach felt bloated. Finally the feeling disappeared, but what seemed as though it were liberating in the beginning was actually a nightmare in disguise. From that point on I found myself in the bathroom 13 or 14 times per day. I couldn't digest any form of food. Suspecting food poisoning, I opted for a visit to my doctor who recommended a diet based on white rice, chicken and steamed zucchini. This was more or less what I would eat for the next ten years of my life. And for a person like me who once thought I would surely end up in the circle of gluttons in hell when I die, this wasn't too easy.

You will discover later on in this book that fortunately neither the devil nor hell exist, and that many issues at first glance seemingly related to cardiological, neurological, dermatological or autoimmune problems are indeed attributable to simple memories. Many of these problems can be resolved very quickly.

In fact, one of my greatest achievements has to do with a gastrointestinal issue. It was with a man named Daniel. Daniel called me a few years ago to make an appointment. When he got to my office, I noticed that for a man only 40 years old his face looked worn. He explained that since the age of eighteen he'd been suffering from a serious ailment that gave him irritation of the colon, though doctors were able to contain it for the first ten years thanks to pharmacological interventions. This ailment recently revealed itself in its most aggressive form.

"You're my last hope," he said with a subdued voice.

I asked if his doctor was aware of our meeting. He said yes. I always ask, because you should never interrupt any treatment recommended by a doctor. I also mentioned that, although past life regressions can often be of great help, they should never be considered an alternative to traditional medicine. I told him that obviously I would do my best. After having fully explained the methodology, I asked him to lie down on the chaise longue. I would put him into a deep state of hypnotic trance. Daniel responded well to the induction technique.

"It's really hot in here, really hot. I almost can't breathe," he began.

I saw that his face was getting redder, he was sweating and he was actually having trouble breathing. This was particularly strange because it was December and the room wasn't hot at all.

His kinesthetic reaction confirmed that he was in a deep state of trance.

"Now I will count from one to three and when I get to three you can breathe normally and you won't feel hot anymore," I said. On three I gently touched his forehead. He began to breathe normally and he stopped sweating.

"Look at your feet, what kind of shoes are you wearing? What kind of material are they? What color?" I asked him.

"They're black boots. I'm a man. I'm in the desert. It's really hot. There is a lot of sand, and it's dark," he continued.

"How are you dressed?" I asked him.

"I'm wearing light canvas pants inserted into my boots. They look white. I'm wearing a uniform. I'm a soldier. I have a rifle… It's old. It has something like a dagger attached to the end of it. Only a few of us are left because there was a battle. Everyone is dead. Only a few of us survived and we're lost in the desert."

"Where are you? In which part of the world?" I asked him.

"I'm in Egypt. I'm French. I come from a small town near the German border and we came to colonize Egypt, with Napoleon."

"What's your name?" I asked.

"My name is François."

"How old are you?"

"28."

"What year is it?"

"1798."

Everything was starting to come together. As I would later discover, Napoleon's Egyptian campaign took place on horseback between 1798 and 1801. It lasted only three years, a seemingly insignificant period in the history of humanity that Daniel had nonetheless managed to identify with precision. After the regression he would tell me that he himself had absolutely no idea in which year the Egyptian campaign took place.

"There are only five of us left," he continued. "I'm on a camel now. Nomads are trying to save us. They're bringing us towards the coast where there's a boat waiting to bring us to Italy, so that we can then go back to France."

"Now I will count from one to five. When I get to five you will automatically move to the most important part of your life," I said to him. "François' life," I added. When I got to five I asked him what was happening and why that moment was so important.

"We're in a big room. It's a court. The room is enormous. The roof seems to be decorated with plaster. The windows are very big. It seems like it's…a military court. All five of us are there. We have military judges in front of us. They're asking us questions. It seems odd to them that we've managed to survive. They think we've deserted. But we're able to explain everything. They don't condemn us. The punishment would have been death."

"I will count from one to three now. On three you will be in the moment of your death. François' death," I said. And I counted.

"I'm about 60 years old," he said. "I feel very weak, very tired. I'm not able to stand up. I fall on the ground easily. I'm sitting in a chair, and my mother is next to me. She is very old. I'm experiencing the after-effects of a debilitating disease that I may have contracted in Egypt."

I went on with the final part of the session and Daniel, like many other people, experienced death and was able to leave behind the suffering that was compromising his quality of life. These symptoms belonged to the existence of François, and for Daniel, they became simple memories of the past. After a few weeks and a few sessions, on one of the happiest days of my life I received a message from Daniel that confirmed that his problems had been substantially reduced and that his life was almost back to normal.

But let's take another step back in time, to my disease. In two years I lost more than 25 kilos. My diet wasn't helping. I would go back to the doctor and he would prescribe me antibiotics but nothing would change. By now four months had passed since I had to ask for leave from work because the frequent breaks I would have to take impeded me from living a normal life. At that time I was living in a small apartment in Milan. I had just gone through a divorce. Ten years of cohabitating had led to a recent wedding in Las Vegas, which at the time I would have described as one of a kind. The divorce, however, happened just as quickly. At that point I was too weak to even go to the supermarket across the street. I'm not recounting all of this to bore the reader with the clinical details of my life, but because it's an important part of the incredible happenings that were about to occur. The state of my health aside, I wasn't a poor soul: the manager's health care plan allowed me to undergo numerous clinical tests. I went to gastroenterologists, endocrinologists, centers for infectious disease and I had gastroscopies and colonoscopies. But nothing. I didn't have anything, but I continued to go to the bathroom and to lose weight. I was still unable to live a normal life. I was reduced to vegetating on the couch most of the time. That was unthinkable for someone like me. As my friend once said, I had experienced more in my life than most people would in three lives. One day I was such a mess that I decided to go back to the emergency room in Milan's Sacco Hospital, center of excellence for gastrointestinal diseases. I would spend all morning there and they would do other tests to then allow me to be seen by one of the most celebrated doctors, whom I won't name. They said that they didn't know what to tell me, that it wasn't possible to make a diagnosis because the exams were negative.

On the way home I was so overtaken by discomfort that I decided to pass by my doctor's office again to ask for more medicine to relieve my symptoms.

And it was there that I met my guardian angel. She was a young doctor named Laura, who was in that day because my regular doctor was on vacation. By coincidence, she was also a gastroenterologist. Today I know there's no such thing as chance, and that any occurrence, even the most simple, is the fruit of the meticulous organization of the universe and of its dynamics. But that day I didn't think anything of it. I described my pitiful condition to her. I watched her think about it for a couple of minutes until she said, "Listen Mr. Raco, if I'm not mistaken it could be a less aggressive form of Crohn's disease. I'll send you to a good doctor in the general hospital for a radiography of your digestive system with a contrast medium."

The word radiography in itself didn't scare me. I thought I was just going to get an X-ray. In reality, though, the following day it would take all the self-control I had not to faint while the doctor completed a procedure on me. She inserted a long tube into my nose that went down through my throat and then continued until my stomach and to the ileum, the initial part of my intestinal tract. I would spend all afternoon sleeping, probably because I was given too great a dose of valium.

I was very surprised to discover the next day when I came back to get the exam that they hadn't administered any anesthesia. The doctor told me that the exam was rather invasive and that I had fallen asleep as a response to the stress. I couldn't understand my body's reaction. At that time, in spite of the four years of psychoanalysis I had undergone as a patient, I still had no knowledge of neurobiology. I quickly went back to Laura's office. After reading the medical report and exams attentively, Laura told me that there was a thickening of the ileum's walls, one of the characteristics of Crohn's disease that couldn't have been diagnosed before because it didn't enter perfectly into clinical parameters. She explained that the other doctors probably didn't realize previously because neither the gastroscopy nor the colonoscopy got to that section of the ileum, a part of the anatomy situated too low to be reached by a gastroscopy but too high to be reached by the colonoscopic pipe. The thickening of the ileum was the origin of my suffering.

I had a diagnosis!

But what now? Laura assured me that the symptoms could be put under control and she prescribed me a specific extended release anti-inflammatory, an absolute novelty at that time. Its gastro-resistant character made it perfect to reach the ileum tract where it could release its beneficial effect. At that time it seemed like the best news I had received since when I still believed in Santa Claus. I wanted to give Laura a big hug and kiss but I limited myself to thanking her and taking my prescription. A few weeks later I was feeling better and started to regain strength, even though I couldn't eat anything besides chicken, white rice and steamed zucchini. Today I know for sure that someone up there made sure Laura was standing in for my regular doctor that day. Chance, as we will see, doesn't exist. After a couple of years of treatment with the anti-inflammatory, my disease was considered to be in a remission state. That means I was more or less able to go about a normal life, with the exception of frequent visits to the bathroom and a diet that did not permit me to commit the sin of gluttony, as it were. In spite of all of this I considered it a miracle. Even though I didn't know at the time that the real miracle, thanks to a hypnotic regression, would come only a few years later.

It was 10 years later, during that dinner at Patrizia and Marco's home, that the events that would radically change my life began to brew.

I responded to Marco's question about my health. I told him that the disease was in remission and that despite my diet, I wasn't too bad. He told me that Patrizia warned him and that he had prepared zucchini as a side dish. He also served me the pasta without sauce.

After dinner, Patrizia invited us to sit down and chat in the living room. While we thought back to the times when her mother was still alive, Patrizia got up and picked up a book from the bookshelf. She passed it to me and said, "Have you read this?" I looked at the cover and read the title *Many Lives, Many Masters*. The author was Dr. Brian Weiss.

I responded no.

"He's a famous American psychiatrist," said Patrizia. "He has a degree in medicine from Columbia University in

New York and he did his specialization at Yale." As if I didn't know, she added, "They are among the ten best universities in the world! And on top of that he is Chairman Emeritus of Psychiatry at the Mount Sinai Medical Center in Miami," she continued. "He works with past life therapy."

"How interesting!" I said, trying to keep a straight face as I laughed.

I thought that my poor friend must have really reached a level of profound desperation owing to the loss of her mother a few months back. My brain struggled to find an explanation for why a person of such scientific esteem as Patrizia would believe in stupid stuff like this.

Throughout all these years, in spite of numerous signs that confirmed the immortality of the conscience and the existence of past lives, I'm still grateful for my brain. That night it allowed me to maintain a scientific and empirical position, even a skeptical one. The subject in itself was already "incredible" and the ability to keep a distance remains, in my view, one of the professional characteristics that whomever dedicates him or herself to the discipline should possess.

Until today, my brain has remained a vigilant scientific observer and has allowed me, time and time again, to be a devil's advocate.

I left saying goodbye and hugged her tight, knowing that I would not be able to see her for another couple of years. I got back into my rental car to drive back to my hotel. As soon as I put the key into the ignition I thought again, "But how is it even possible that people actually believe in these crazy stories? She has to be in serious despair."

I didn't know how wrong I was!

One night, I was back home in Barcelona and wasting time in front of the computer. That conversation on past lives I had with Patrizia came back to me. I was worried for my friend: Who was that doctor with these strange theories that she was so interested in? I decided to investigate as I wanted to understand what would have convinced Patrizia to believe in these absurdities. I searched for Dr. Brian Weiss's website and I checked his academic and professional credentials myself. I was pretty surprised. I thought he would be an unscrupulous person who wanted to get rich by taking advantage of grieving individuals like my friend.

I also saw his face for the first time and thought that he didn't at all seem like one of those typical guys whose image created by marketing is able to hoodwink the masses. "But how can people like Patrizia believe in such nonsense," I thought again. From the perspective of a business and marketing manager, I had a hard time believing how a simple-looking person, let alone someone who looked like Dr. Weiss, could have been able to sell millions of books all over the world and have hundreds of thousands of followers from all walks of life. I wasn't truly astonished, however, until I saw that his only event scheduled in Europe that year was a seminar in Barcelona, exactly five days later. I thought it was a strange coincidence. The website explained that there would also be a book signing. I decided to go, to get a book dedicated to Patrizia, and to get to the bottom of this. Anyway, in the worst case scenario I could also have a few laughs at those "poor fools," I thought. I bought a ticket and five days later I was in line with another hundred or so people waiting to see this "guru" up close. When it was my turn Dr. Weiss came close to me, smiled, and shook my hand. He looked like just an average guy in front of me, devoid of that arrogance that seemed to accompany others like him. He was a man who, despite his fame, and despite the fact that he sold millions of books, seemed devoid of an ego. Upon closer look, he emanated charisma and energy through his two bright eyes, and an almost supernatural placidity.

I returned home with an odd sensation of peacefulness.

It must have been that sensation that convinced me to come back the next morning for the second part of the seminar. I was seated in the audience of an enormous conference center in the Catalan capital with another thousand people. Dr. Weiss was inviting guests to get comfortable on the stage to participate in a group past life regression. I decided to participate in order to prove to myself that there wasn't anything true about what he was claiming. I could suspend my criticism about the doctor but I still couldn't accept his theories. I looked around and I couldn't help but judge the poor people who found themselves there. I looked at them with a mixture of pity and criticism. For me they were poor, suffering people in search of any explanation that would alleviate their pain. They were people who would eat up all kinds of nonsense.

I closed my eyes and let myself go. And what I saw with my own eyes confirmed for me that nothing had been further from the truth.

ALEX OR SOPHIE?

My arms started to move by themselves, nervously, while I sat with my eyes closed on an armchair in the Barcelona Forum, an enormous conference center with more than one thousand seats. The fingertips on both of my hands were moving back and forth on my thighs, up and down, rhythmically and repeatedly. They were doing it on their own.

"What the hell is happening?" I thought, confused and slightly scared. I couldn't stop my arms. They continued to move by themselves.

I looked down towards my feet, following the instructions of Dr. Weiss as he guided all one thousand participants from the stage. He was using progressive relaxation, one of the few hypnotic techniques able to induce a large quantity of people simultaneously into a moderate trance without any collateral effects. It is a very relaxing and pleasant technique that I use quite often, very similar to a guided meditation.

While I was trying to focus my gaze towards the ground, my feet finally appeared. I was wearing black shoes, rounded at the toes, and white tights. They were the shoes of a child. My brain, normally very present and analytical, was taken by surprise this time. I wasn't daydreaming.

I turned my head to the right and in front of my eyes were the walls of a grey building made up of stone slabs. It was a refined building of several floors with a large black door, rounded at the top, with enormous, shiny, silver door knockers. My gaze lingered on those door knockers because they were extremely familiar to me. The windows were white, enormous and void of shutters. This was my house, without a doubt. I lived here, in London. I knew that I was six years old, that it was 1812 and that my name was Sophie. All of this in what seemed like less than a second. I couldn't believe what was happening to me.

"You're just making this up, you're making everything up," My mind kept telling me. But I had the clear-cut sensation that the information I had received and the images I was seeing were not a product of my own mind. I felt like they were coming from an external source. They came to me too quickly and spontaneously to be the fruit of my own imagination. They seemed more like memories.

Today I know for sure that they were not a figment of my imagination. In order to imagine something, the brain needs the fractions of a second necessary to elaborate on an "invention," whereas memories surface instantaneously. And that was exactly what was happening to me, I was receiving a large amount of information with the absolute certainty that I was the subject.

When people come to my office, one of the methodologies that I normally use to ascertain whether the information coming to them is memory or imagination is evaluating the immediacy of their responses. Basically, I don't allow their brain the time to imagine anything. If the information comes instantly I believe that is major proof that we're dealing with memories of a past life.

People expect to see something. We live in a world where optical stimuli are predominant. Out of our five senses, vision is undoubtedly the one we use the most. This means that if we are expecting to experience a past life, we want images. In order to avoid false or exaggerated expectations, I normally explain that it is actually impossible to "see" anything. I guide people through a process of how to collect information or feelings from their own experience, things that then need to be processed by their mind in order to be understood. The eyes are like biological cameras that send images to the brain through our optic nerves. Therefore, if the eyelids are closed, as is the case during hypnosis, it becomes impossible to see. In spite of this, there are some people who have extremely detailed visual experiences during a regression. This is not the case for me.

The only "supernatural" experience of my life before that moment was just a few minutes earlier, when Brian had conducted a psychometric exercise. I say "Brian" because Dr. Weiss wants to be called only by his given name, despite having sold millions of books and having changed the lives of millions of people. I volunteered to participate in this exercise simply because I didn't want to stand out. Everyone around me was doing it. Obviously at that point I still believed that it was a scam. The exercise was done in pairs and consisted of receiving information during a state of light meditation while holding an object that belonged to another one of the participants. Not knowing the other person, you wouldn't have had any way to know the information being transmitted to you. My left hemisphere, the most rational part of the brain, continued to mock me, my partner, and all of the poor aspiring psychics in the room. My partner was a young man sitting right behind me. He handed over his cellphone. It was an object he would always carry with him without a shadow of a doubt. I closed my eyes and let myself be guided.

During the exercise I perceived that the cellphone in my hands was expanding and little by little, taking the shape of a ball. The ball was slightly elongated at the ends. You can't imagine my surprise, and that of my rational brain, when at the end of the exercise the guy told me that he played professional football for more than 15 years. Football, or "American football," as we call it in Europe, is not at all popular on this side of the Atlantic. "What a coincidence!" I thought.

I still hadn't discovered yet that coincidences do not exist.

Those who undergo a past life regression can have substantially different experiences from one another. Some have purely visual experiences with different levels of detail, whereas others have dreamlike experiences. Those with dreamlike experiences go through past events in the same way in which one normally dreams. These people are able to clearly perceive only a few details at a time even if they are absolutely aware of what is going on around them, as if they were watching a scene through a telescope. Other people have kinesthetic experiences, as in corporeal sensations such as heat, cold or even movements, like my arms at the Forum.

Looking back with a clear head, I now know that during my regression that day, I was having both a dreamlike and kinesthetic experience.

I looked down again and tried to concentrate my attention on my shoes. I saw that I was wearing a long, grey, poofy dress that went down to my knees. I couldn't see my face but I had the sensation of having blonde, wavy hair. I was wearing a white bonnet on my head. I was seated high above the floor, and I realized that I could see the building to my right through a small window. It was a car window, I thought at first. Then I immediately understood that it was actually a carriage. In front of me there was a wooden seat with a dark grey cover similar to velvet, with buttons. Through the small window I was able to see a golden lamp that was hanging from the edge of the top of the carriage. All of this information was coming to me in fractions of a second, at an unimaginable speed for the normal capacity of my brain. I never considered myself to be stupid, but compared to this new speed my old brain functions were irritatingly slow.

At the time I wasn't aware of this, but in the past fifteen years, many studies on the brain have demonstrated that during a meditation or a state of hypnotic trance, many neuronal areas become activated that stay dormant in our normal state of consciousness. These studies have been possible thanks to neuroimaging instruments such as MRI (magnetic resonance imaging) or PET (positron emission tomography). The hypnotic trance, as will be explained later on in this book, is similar to what one experiences in a regression. I'm not trying to bore anyone with detailed notions of neuroanatomy, so I will just say this: During hypnosis, in the frontal part of the brain, regional cerebral blood flow increases. At the same time, a decrease in the connective functionality of the lateral frontoparietal system is observed. If we consider that the first of the two, the frontal part of the cerebral cortex, is the one where it is thought that consciousness resides while the second, the lateral frontoparietal system, receives external sensorial stimuli, everything seems clearer, even to a layman. During a meditative or hypnotic state the importance of external stimuli decreases progressively and at the same time you are able to access a state of hyperconsciousness. What I was experiencing in that moment, without knowing it, had to be a state of hyperconsciousness.

The quantity of the information that I was receiving was far superior to my brain's capacity for elaboration of data. In one of the following chapters I will talk more in detail about our brain and the role of consciousness. For now I will only say that at the time it was as if I had connected a fiber optic USB data transfer cable to a computer from the eighties.

Sophie's life—my life—came to me in detail in only a couple of seconds.

I apologize to the reader if I'm digressing, but my purpose is to explain exactly what happens during regression therapy, when interferences from the rational left hemisphere continue to interrupt and wander while a part of the subconscious, apparently uncontrollable and unknown, takes the lead. And my left brain, for better or for worse, was always extremely present, practical and rational. Even today, after many years, it continues to fight me and to remain skeptical. To have faith is always the easiest part; the difficult thing is remaining skeptical while keeping an open mind. It's always fun when people come into my office and expect to meet some sort of psychic medium, given the supernatural theme they associate with past lives. So I let my left brain speak and explain to them that I don't possess any type of psychic ability. I do my job, I say. I try to do it well, but I am only a technician. I apply a technique that allows the conscious mind to connect with the soul and to receive information regarding another existence. And this is what normally happens during a regression, as I myself was experiencing in that moment at the Barcelona Forum.

I then looked to my left. Sitting on the folding seat of the carriage next to me was a woman, roughly 30 years old. She seemed so tall to me, but it was only because I was a small child. She too wore a bonnet, but hers was dark and more rigid. I had never seen that type of clothing before. It seemed like a uniform. I wasn't able to see her face too well so I concentrated on her dress. It was also grey, but of a much darker shade than mine, a color that nowadays, ironic as it is, we call "London smoke." From the window of the carriage I saw the grey sky and a sort of mist that filled the street, not allowing me to see very far. I didn't know if the fog was the fruit of my imagination, a product of my brain's difficulty in visualizing this past life, or if it was real fog. It was London so certainly any of the three was plausible. I turned to look at the woman sitting next to me. She had an austere but maternal air about her. I thought maybe she was my mom. But something inside of me was suggesting otherwise. She was wearing dark gloves and her hands were chubby, totally the opposite of my small hands, which appeared tapered, clean and of a very white complexion. I also saw my nails, small and perfect, the nails of a child. The woman next to me was my nanny. Now it was clear to me. Her shoes captured my attention. They were short boots with pewter buttons, perfectly cleaned. I thought that we must have been very rich, judging by the clothes that my nanny and I were wearing. And also judging by the people I could see while looking out the window. They were all impeccably dressed, both women and men. In the meantime, the carriage had abandoned the main road where we lived and I could see a few people walking on the sidewalk. The women were wearing long gowns and the men were wearing top hats, some very tall. They seemed very elegant.

We were now in the city center, it seemed. The street was dusty, given the enormous number of carriages and pedestrians. These people weren't wearing fancy clothes; some were even dressed very modestly, their outfits more like rags. I felt out of place and at the same time a little bit guilty. Those people were barely surviving in a respectable manner and I, even at my young age, knew that I was very wealthy. I looked at my nanny again inside the carriage and I was finally able to see her face, plump and covered by numerous freckles. She had small lips but a very affectionate and maternal expression. She sweetly caressed my face. Following Brian's instructions, I looked into her blue eyes and was able to perceive her soul. In that moment it was totally clear. She had my aunt's soul. My aunt from this present life.

Though confused at first, I realized within a couple of seconds that my aunt Marisa's soul had been with me since the beginning of the regression into this past life. I called her "aunt," but in reality she was my mother's dearest friend. She's been gone for a few years now. She was a person who, like my beloved nanny, had accompanied me through childhood only to leave me when my path became steady. Looking back with a clear head, when I connected the dots, I found it funny that my aunt Marisa had actually surprised me with a trip to London for my sixteenth birthday. Just the two of us in London.

Then, looking my aunt in the eyes, I could understand why my soul decided to show me this life. I got one of the messages I was supposed to receive: "Do what you want to do, always and in every moment." These words resounded in my mind like a message coming from an unearthly dimension.

In fact, my aunt lived quite a complicated existence. She was diagnosed with cancer at only 20 years old and she went through surgery many times. She passed away at 57, and according to her surgeon, she was one of the longest surviving patients of this type of pathology. Despite the illness, she was a very active and determined woman. She traveled all over the world and her disease never stopped her. She was a living example of the fact that we need to live in the present, every moment to our highest potential, without worrying about the future or feeling guilty about the past.

Do what you want to do, always and in every moment. Exactly.

Curiously, at least for me at that time, my nanny didn't look anything like my aunt Marisa. My aunt was a tiny woman, certainly not fat, with auburn hair and greenish brown eyes. It didn't look like her because it wasn't her. It was only her soul.

Throughout my experience with over 16 of my own regressions and the hundreds of people I have been able to induce into hypnosis, I have learned that our souls decide to come to Earth to learn lessons. They plan everything out before we are born. They know perfectly well from the beginning what will happen to them during life on Earth. Even if, at times, lessons can appear extremely difficult or painful, our souls choose these roles, this existence. Humans suffer but souls know no suffering. As Dr. Brian Weiss has so finely explained in his books, with a narrative capability that made him the leading expert in the field of past lives, our human life is somewhat similar to a theatrical play. Our soul is the actor and the human being is the protagonist. At the end of the show, the actor goes home, satisfied and happy with his or her performance, even if that involved suffering or even a violent death during the play. The soul, finished with its earthly existence, returns home and frees itself of any type of suffering.

Often people ask me if hell exists, and I say yes. Hell exists on Earth, and we can realize that just by looking at the suffering that surrounds us. In the afterlife there is no suffering. Only love is real, the only energy which unites us all. It is a form of energy very different from that which we experience here on Earth. It is unconditional, infinite love. This is what everyone I guide into regression describes to me. I've encountered all types of people, among them some who were problematic, depressed, negative, and even a few who followed voodoo rituals. But all of them, without exception, have felt this unconditional love during the regression. No one has ever encountered devils or evil spirits of any form.

Our souls travel in time, throughout numerous existences, in groups of large families composed of many members. My aunt was my nanny during my life as Sophie. Our souls travel together to help one another learn the love that surrounds us. It's as simple as it gets.

Brian then guided us to the most important moment of the existence that we all were simultaneously experiencing, but in separate lives. My hands began to move again, by themselves, back and forth along my thighs. A feeling of anxiety grew inside of me. I couldn't see anything and I was breathing heavily, or at least that's what I thought, because during a hypnotic trance you may feel sensations greater than what is actually occurring in your body.

I saw blood. Little by little images started to appear. Then, all of the information came suddenly, in a fraction of a second. I was spread out, half lying down on a bed, in an enormous room. The windows were big and tall, the same ones that I saw from the outside, while inside the carriage. I was in my house, in my bedroom. To my right, my nanny was sitting in a chair. She was worried, but she looked at me with a combination of love and reassurance. She had white bandages in her hands, and they were moist. From that look I understood that I wasn't dying. My nanny appeared much older than before. She was a woman in her fifties. The few wrinkles that surrounded her blue eyes revealed the age of her plump face. She had more freckles and this time they covered her entire face. She was dressed more or less in the same way, with a long, dark, grey gown, poofy at the bottom but tight around the waist. But she was not wearing a bonnet. Her white hair, once blonde, was up in a bun. I myself was a 30-year-old woman. It was 1836. I don't know where this information came from, but it came to me with a clarity and speed that made it unequivocal. The bed would be gigantic in comparison to a bed from today. It was made of strong, brown wood with flower engravings. I clearly saw my legs covered by a white nightgown, embroidered with quality fabric. It was covered in blood.

Blood was covering my entire pelvis and part of my legs, tinting the white nightgown red. My hands moved furiously back and forth along my thighs, scraping my flesh through the fabric. The pain was unbearable. I cried and screamed. I was having a miscarriage.

My brain was in stand-by. That experience was really outside of any conscious control of the imagination. How was it possible that I, Alex, a forty-something manager with a prestigious degree and a long, brilliant career behind me, was seeing myself as Sophie, a thirty-something woman in the middle of a miscarriage—170 years earlier?

I had already climbed all the ladders of a brilliant career in high-level multinational companies, starting with Procter & Gamble, then Sara Lee, Walt Disney and Stepstone. By then I was ready to take on the position of General Manager of a large company. I had just moved to Barcelona for a sabbatical and was sifting through the employment ads of numerous companies. I was living in a beautiful penthouse with a wooden terrace with a view of the sea, in one of the nicest neighborhoods. I had a stable, loving relationship that lasted more than six years. My Mercedes Cabriolet was parked in the garage underneath my house. I went to the most exclusive gym in the center of the city. I had just passed the theory portion of my private pilot license, with numerous flying hours in the Barcelona area. My life consisted of dinners out, trips and constant fun. I had everything that a man my age could ever want. What did Sophie and I have in common?

Nothing. None of my early partners had ever miscarried. I don't have sisters and in my own home I had never seen anything of the sort. Nothing.

Before that day, if someone asked me whether I believed in past lives, I would have thought they had a screw loose. If I had to imagine a past life, I would have probably thought of a musketeer in the Louis XIV's palace. Definitely not the life of Sophie and her—my miscarriage.

That day I finally understood a strange sensation I had felt in past years, during my frequent business trips. Déjà vu. That slight repulsion that I felt every time I got on a direct flight to London, despite getting along well with the English, who have always been very nice to me and with whom I share a part of my culture. Every time I went to London, at that time every week, I had an overpowering sensation of discomfort. I was sad even when it was sunny. The enormous buildings, though renowned and beautiful, instilled a fear in me. There was something not right in that wonderful, cosmopolitan, and lively city. I could feel a negative aura, like a filter that would obscure all vitality and positivity. I had always asked myself why a place with such lovely attractions, the monuments, the retro style, the humour, could give me such an unpleasant feeling. I had always attributed those feelings to a dissatisfaction with my work schedule and the responsibility and stress of my managerial position. It was a dissatisfaction that even in the nicest periods of my life gave me a handful of behavioral problems. Today I can be grateful for that dissatisfaction. I know that it represented an alarm signal to my brain: There was something in my life that wasn't going well, no matter how perfect it appeared. After a tireless night in which I inspected my annual expenditures in clothing, trips and amusement with my platinum card, which amounted to the cost of a studio apartment in Milan these days, I decided that it was time to end this madness. I asked for the help of a famous psychiatrist in Milan, a professor at the University of Urbino. I entered one of the most wonderful stages of my life: four and a half years of psychoanalytic sessions, twice a week. Besides making me a decidedly better person, these sessions gave me a solid base to take on my profession with serenity and preparation.

On the left of the bed, covered in Sophie's blood, were two men. The first had shaved white hair and he was around 40 years old. Honestly, he didn't look too great. He had minuscule, metal, oval glasses that were almost round. He had small, bright brown eyes. He was wearing a white shirt with a Korean collar and some strange pants equipped with a large back flap, closed with four buttons, two on each side. The sleeves of his shirt were rolled up. He was my doctor. He was trying to save me from the worst. He repeated to the others in the room that everything was going to be okay.

Just behind him, off to the side, there was another man. He was younger and very attractive. He had dark, thick, wavy hair and long, wide, sideburns. His complexion was clear and his wonderful, deep blue eyes stood out. His features were perfect. His nose was straight but substantial, and he had a proportionate but commanding jaw. He was tall and dressed very nicely. Straight leg pants brought out his slim legs and his tight shirt revealed a strong body.

His name was John and he was my husband. Sophie's husband. He was an important businessman, a banker. Thanks to him we were very wealthy and could live in a big house. We met at a high society event. I still remember how he looked at me and the feelings that he brought on in the young woman that I was at that time. It was a mix of love and protection, strength and passion. On my end it was love at first sight. I decided to abandon myself to these feelings and to live with him for the rest of my life. His eyes conquered me. Our relatives were not opposed to our marriage. In fact, they had everything to gain. I was a descendant of a noble family but our finances were slowly but surely depleting; his family was very wealthy and desired a prestigious place in society. So we got married with a lavish and elegant ceremony with ample social appeal.

There, at that moment in my bedroom, his gaze contained both love and disapproval. Disappointment shone through those deep blue eyes that at other times expressed an indescribable vitality and could show me the strongest and most sincere love.

His heir—my son—would never be born.

A sensation of deep sorrow, inadequacy, and abandonment took over me. I no longer cared. I was burnt out. Total emptiness. I wanted to die. Even my nanny's sweet gaze could not compete with those cold, blue eyes that were full of disappointment. Within just a few moments

I simultaneously lost my first child and the person who I loved most on the face of the earth.

Continuing to follow Brian's instructions, I distanced myself from the experience and observed it from afar as if it were a film. Immediately, as if it were magic, the feelings of atrocious pain and sadness were reduced. I was only left with the desire to know, without any physical or emotional involvement. Basically, I knew how I was feeling but I didn't feel that way firsthand. Soon happiness would accompany the other feelings. Despite knowing that my husband had ignored me, physically and emotionally, I knew I would see my son again. I knew in an instant that inside my son, the baby who would never be born, was the soul of Alex's brother. My brother's soul!

I knew that he would stay with me, that he would come back. I knew that I would be able to hug him and love him. A sensation of indescribable love came over my entire body. Now I can understand the unique ties I have with my brother. He's 45 years old, a husband, a father, and manager of a well-known publicly owned company. He's similar to me in every way. But despite him being an independent adult, in my eyes he will always be a child in need of protection. We live in two different countries but we speak daily, by phone or video chat. I couldn't live without him. And after that day, this was even clearer. The universe brought him back to me and in the best form possible, that of a brother, and my ties to him are indissoluble by nature. It was as if to compensate for Sophie's suffering, I was given nothing less than pure joy for all of these years. It was a divine gift.

We were then guided to another phase in that life, thanks to Brian's calm voice. I saw myself on a street in central London, Knightsbridge. I had just gotten off my family's carriage and I was crossing the street to go shopping in a new, large store that had recently opened. I then discovered that it was *Harrods*, at the time that it had moved to Knightsbridge. I was holding hands with my three girls, two to my right and the smallest one to my left. We all walked together, one parallel to the next. We were dressed in luxury clothing. The refined fabric of the long, velvet dresses came down almost to our feet. I felt ample joy and excitement in that moment. It was one of the rare moments of happiness that Sophie's life had after the miscarriage. John and I had three beautiful girls that I loved deeply. They gave me a reason to live. Every day they gave me the happiness that, in some way, seemed to stop up the emptiness left by my disinterested husband. He was also disinterested in our daughters, whom he never gave much attention. Don't get me wrong, he never neglected his responsibilities towards them. They grew up comfortably, surrounded by every type of luxury. But they were never loved. They never got a hug or a compliment. Our family did not give him what he desired. We would not have a male heir. The oldest of my daughters walked on my right side, giving me her hand. She was nine years old and she had dark, wavy hair like her dad. She was pretty tall for her age and she was extremely responsible. She took care of her little sisters as if she were a little mom. By simply looking down at her from my height while we were crossing Knightsbridge, I knew that I recognized her soul. I, Alex, knew who she was.

My child had the soul of my aunt Maria Luisa, my father's sister in my current life. Even though I wasn't able to see her much when I became an adult, she took care of me when I was a small child. Curiously, she did the same 150 years ago with her little sisters, Sophie's children. In a picture that I looked at recently, I was a just a newborn in her arms. The way that we looked at one another was unequivocal. Our souls have known each other forever. And I had known it already after only having lived a few days. My gaze in that photo seemed to be telling her, "Here I am, my little one. I'm back. We're together again."

The middle sister holding my right hand was not a soul present in my current life. But that doesn't mean that the love that I felt for her in that moment, and even still today, is insignificant. I know that my soul knows hers. We're part of the same celestial family and I will probably come back to meet her in another life as a sister, brother, father, son, grandmother, niece... Who knows? We are born many times because we learn many lessons on Earth. Only in experiencing all possible roles can our souls grow, become stronger, and fill themselves with energy and infinite love.

The youngest one, who held my left hand as we walked, was almost four years old. Her hair was blonde like mine, with loose curls. She had a round and freckly face and two enormous blue eyes that gazed up at me, full of love. I knew her. Her soul was familiar. Looking in her deep blue eyes I understood that inside my child was my aunt Maria Antonietta's soul, the sister of Alex's mother. Another aunt?

An analyst would surely say at this point that I must be obsessed with aunts. Having gotten to know myself profoundly through my current occupation, I can say that that's not the case. I was very surprised during the regression, another element that validated that I wasn't making anything up. If I had to invent a past life, I can assure you that I wouldn't have involved any of my aunts. In any case, throughout the years, and during several more past life regressions, I met my aunt Maria Antonietta many times, always in the form of a girl. But I don't want to bore the reader with irrelevant personal information. I will limit myself to saying that I had always considered her my favorite aunt. Now I understand that our souls are forever connected and that we will come back with the same roles as close family, to help one another during our numerous existences. Soul mates.

As we will discover, soulmates can appear in many different roles in our lives. In any case, and regardless of the nature and duration of the relationship, they are always very important roles.

Following the expert guiding voice of Brian, I went to the last moments of Sophie's existence. I was in the same bed where I had miscarried 36 years earlier. I was now 66 years old. The enormous window to my right allowed a lot of light into the room. This was something unusual for London, a luxury that only the wealthy could benefit from. I immediately understood that John had continued to be my husband for the remainder of my life and that he had always guaranteed me a luxurious life. But he had never loved me. Our relationship had been solidly social and familial, but not loving. In fact, he wasn't there in the room with me that day, the day of my death. He was off on one of his business trips that became more and more frequent as time went on. The trips had always kept him far from me and his daughters. The daughters were there, all around my bed. I recognized them immediately as Maria Antonietta and Maria Luisa. I will call them by my aunt's names as I haven't had the possibility to discover their names in that past life. They had become splendid women. They were still luxuriously dressed and groomed. The looks on their faces were sad, and tears came down from their wonderful eyes. I knew that as mother and children we had a wonderful relationship, filled with love. They were my jewels, my pride, my strength. I didn't want to leave them. Two waiters in grey uniforms with aprons went back and forth in the enormous bedroom, busily, but there was no trace of my beloved nanny. She had left us a few years back, but in that moment I knew that her body was resting in our large noble tomb as the indispensable member of our family that she was.

I had a cold and my strength was abandoning me. Brian counted from one to three. And on three I learned what it meant to die.

My soul left my body and I could observe the scene from above. The physical sensation that I felt in that moment was indescribable. It wasn't a human sensation, as anyone who I've treated can tell you. You abandon your physical state and you feel a kind of love that has no equivalent for earthly beings. Physical pain, as well as the emotional pain tied to having to leave your loved ones from that life, disappear within a few seconds. A profound peace takes its place. But this peace is actually eternal, in the sense that it goes beyond the human conception of time.

I abandoned Sophie and our life. I looked at her with tenderness and infinite love, knowing that she was, and continues to be, a part of me. I was leaving the suffering and sadness that had accompanied her during her life and taking with me, in our soul, the love for our children and the important lessons that her life had promised me.

First of all, there was the gift of having found my children in the form of a beloved brother and three sweet and ever-present aunts. Then, I realized that the fact that I didn't have children in this life, in Alex's life, was nothing other than a gift from God or from the Universe (you choose what to call the wonderful energy of pure love of which we are all made). After the suffering caused by the miscarriage and by Sophie's loveless life, I understood that Alex's existence represents a break that allowed me to dedicate my time and my energy to another kind of love, one that I give to others.

"You have to dedicate yourself to helping others." That sentence resounded through a telepathic voice that bypassed my ears and went straight to my consciousness. It spread like energy and could be understood directly by my entire being, my essence, my soul.

Next to me I clearly perceived two celestial presences made of light. At the time I didn't know it, but they were what Brian calls Masters. It was as if they were looking at me, smiling at me, holding my hand, hugging me, and permeating me all at once. They made me feel a love that even today I have difficulty putting into words.

I left the Barcelona Forum's conference center that night with the clear-cut, unequivocal feeling that nothing that I had experienced was just my imagination. I didn't have the slightest idea how much my life had changed that day! I remember the next morning I was eating breakfast on the terrace with my usual American coffee and a bagel with cream cheese and jam, a habit that I brought with me from my younger days in the United States. As I sat under the gigantic umbrella that sheltered me from the amazing Barcelona sun, I had completely lost any fear of death.

In the two following weeks all of the symptoms of my disease, Crohn's disease, had disappeared. Even though it was in remission, it had still accompanied me throughout all my days until then. I started, little by little, to eat everything again, without experiencing any collateral damage. And today, after many years, I continue to eat everything without experiencing any symptoms. I came to understand, to my amazement, that my disease, characterized by strong pain in my lower stomach, had afflicted me simply due to memories that I brought with me throughout the centuries. They were memories of Sophie's suffering, of the miscarriage and of the loss of her son. My son.

Because my soul could experience that feeling again and could understand the origin of the suffering through regression, my body was freed. I was astonished. I started to talk about it with everyone, even though at that time the topic was little-known, despite Dr. Weiss's efforts, and most people took me for a crazy person. This was exactly what I had done with my poor friend Patrizia and with the participants of Brian's seminar. Now I know that I was the ignorant one.

My materialistic and profoundly earthly existence up to that point was about to change, because I was newly aware: I wasn't supposed to dedicate all of my energy to myself egotistically, but I had to dedicate it to others. Within a couple of weeks, I decided to abandon my managerial career to accept a job with much lower pay, and with fewer responsibilities. I was able to do this thanks to my savings, the help of my parents and the cost of living in Barcelona, which was not comparable to Milan's high prices. I rented a small, modest apartment. I quit my pilot lessons. I replaced my car with a used motor scooter. I started to go to a communal gym and I decreased my dining budget by inviting my few dear friends to my home. I realized that what was really important in life was not material goods. By drastically reducing the cost of my lifestyle, I could finally have more free time to dedicate to myself and to others, just as my celestial guides had suggested.

I started to learn more about psychology and psychotherapy. I went to more of Brian Weiss's seminars and I underwent a series of past life regressions with Emanuela, my friend from Rome whom Brian had recommended. I even started to go to a Buddhist center where I learned about meditation and mindfulness. I don't consider myself Buddhist in the strict sense of the word, but I now live in a manner coherent with Buddha's philosophy from many points of view.

My new studies took up almost all of time. I lived for them above all else. A surprising force that I didn't understand had given me a push and the willingness to continue, so much so that I decided to register for a postgraduate diploma in anxiety and mood disorders, a program normally reserved to doctors and clinical psychologists. However, the knowledge that I had acquired by teaching myself and the years I had spent undergoing psychoanalysis allowed me to complete it successfully. I still remember, now with nostalgia, that my first afternoons and nights dedicated to studying neurobiology made me so afraid to fail that I was brought to tears with rage and desperation.

But I wasn't alone. Now I know that I had superhuman help. I was determined to seriously take on the material so I started a hypnosis course for beginners. I also enrolled in a professional university training in clinical hypnosis in Madrid. Thanks to my graduate studies in psychology, I had no problem getting in. It was the right choice because the program was organized by one of the most well-known experts in clinical hypnosis in all of Spain, a profoundly competent university professor and a real authority on the subject. The first day of the course I asked him about past life regression hypnosis and he seemed skeptical. I decided not to talk about it anymore, understanding his point of view: the academic world was already very closed when it comes to clinical hypnosis, let alone past life regression. Nevertheless, some of the knowledge that I was able to acquire from him has contributed to my daily practice and remains a valid complement to the methodology of Brian Weiss, which I follow during my sessions.

Nothing in life is a coincidence. Now I know that all of the things that happened to me up until that point were preliminary. They were like small pieces of a puzzle that don't represent anything on their own but that together can produce an image of dazzling beauty. My education and my far-flung upbringing allowed me to speak four languages fluently. In this way, I was able to help a large number of people. I am profoundly grateful to the universe and I like to think that this is the gift that this life had in store for me.

Still today, I find the radical change in my life incredible, and I find it incredible how little effort was required on my part. I went from a life centered upon pleasure, spending, luxury and egoism to an almost monastic life. I went from an apartment that could have been featured in a magazine to a minuscule studio apartment, and from a Mercedes to a small used motor scooter. Was this really me? The successful manager with a Master's Degree in Business Administration that everyone knew?

I had a new soul. During my last trip to New York, where I went for professional past life regression therapy training with Brian Weiss and his wife Carole, I had an additional experience that indicated that a profound change had taken place in my existence. I only allow myself to travel economy, and I look back on my trips as a manager in business and first class without nostalgia. The airplane seats in economy are equipped with personal entertainment screens. I was watching *The Best Exotic Marigold Hotel*, a charming film with Maggie Smith in which the protagonists, a group of older English people, decide to move to India because their retirement funds don't allow them to live a decent life in England. The person next to me was watching an American film in which a billionaire from Beverly Hills drove a flaming red Ferrari. I recognized myself and felt a strange serenity and happiness while watching the decrepit rooms of the Marigold Hotel, whereas I felt a strange repulsion when confronted with the luxurious car and Beverly Hills home. Was it really me?

When I reached New York, the city that educated me more than any other and where I had the fortune of living as an adolescent, it was confirmed. New York seemed sad, chaotic, nervous and inconclusive compared to my previous time there. What had happened in New York? Nothing, absolutely nothing. It was the same wonderful metropolis as always. I was the one who had changed. The people who walked the streets in a hurry appeared to me, for the first time, like beings without souls who were running towards a goal that they themselves didn't know. The goal was a material illusion that only one out of a million can reach, only to discover that it doesn't bring them happiness. For years I was like them, but now I saw them as slaves for the first time. They were prisoners of a brutal mechanism, asleep on the metro after too many hours of work trying to pay an excessive rent, just to be able to participate in an enormous lottery in which the prize was unknown. Now I could never live there. I was the one who had changed. New York will always be that vibrant city, full of positive energy, that has welcomed me time and time again, inspired me and redirected me. Indeed, the city that never sleeps. The melting pot of races and cultures, where everyone can meet their own dimension. It's a magic place that holds the memories of my youth. No need for me to judge.

Thanks to the experiences of the many people that conceded me the privilege of their trust, thanks to their regressions—some of which are described in this book—I realized that every one of us has our own path, and in order to learn, we all have to have as many experiences as possible. We have to be women, men, white, black, Asian, Christian, Muslim, Jewish, Buddhist, Hindu, atheist, straight, gay, rich, poor... this is why we come to Earth. We come to learn. This is our school.

"There is nothing either good or bad, but thinking makes it so." (Shakespeare, when Hamlet speaks to Rosencrantz). And nothing is either right or wrong, but our mind makes it so.

HYPNOSIS AND MYTHS

I met Adrian on a sunny and mild late September day, one of those perfect Barcelona days that feel like summer but without the humidity or excessive heat. That day, I had time to reflect on that pleasantly mild weather while I waited for the train at the station of the coastal town I was fortunate enough to live in, and then again as I walked the distance that separates the train station from my office. Just one week prior, wearing a heavy shirt and walking along the sunny streets had seemed like torture.

Adrian had just entered my office when I got in. He was about 40 years old, tall and thin with black, wavy hair. He wore metal-framed glasses, oval-shaped, which made him seem much less attractive than he was. He had a long thin nose, small, almost almond-shaped and with very expressive eyes. He wore a pair of grey jeans and a long-sleeved white shirt. I shook his hand to welcome him and noticed that he was sweaty. Once we were sitting down, I noticed with surprise his shirt, which was dotted all over with huge sweat stains. Adrian excused himself, blaming the excessive summer heat. But it was a lovely September day, not exactly hot and humid. And if a slightly overweight person such as myself could appreciate the fresh, dry air, there was no way that a thin man such as Adrian could have sweat that much because of the heat.

I wasn't wrong. If Adrian was sweating, it wasn't because of the Barcelona weather. His hands trembled as he told me the reason for his visit. His face was flushed, and he constantly avoided eye contact.

I always try to make the people who come to do a regression feel at ease. I smile, I try to show empathy and I always maintain, at the beginning of a session, a friendly demeanor. But with Adrian it was impossible to establish such a rapport. He told me about his depression, his anhedonia (inability to find pleasure in any activities), low self-esteem, lack of appetite, and insomnia. Recently, all this had also been accompanied by panic attacks with an elevated heart rate and difficulty breathing, crises that were becoming more and more intense. The incidents became more frequent the year before, upon the death of his grandfather, with whom he was very close.

The father of two children on the brink of adolescence, Adrian had recently gotten a divorce. He told me that he was experiencing a sort of psychological block every time he was alone with the children. This began to create problems for him, because he often found himself having to take care of the children without his ex-wife. When I asked him to tell me about the relationship he had with his father, he said it had always been contentious, since he was about seven or eight years old.

He told me that in the past he had suffered from a major depression disorder diagnosed as a clinical depression with comorbid anxiety as a secondary symptom. Anxiety is a symptom that accompanies many psychological problems. People often say they suffer from anxiety, even if most of the time this isn't the main problem at the root of their malaise. It constitutes an alarm bell, a symptom that can often indicate the presence of another problem.

"I don't know anything about your technique, Mister Raco," he said to me. "I come to you at the recommendation of my friend who knows you and has already done regressions with you."

Hearing those words I immediately understood the reason behind the nervousness, the tremors, and the sweating.

"Adrian, what do you know about hypnosis?" I asked him.

"I'm not sure," he said. "I believe that it happens like in movies or on television, you'll say some words and I'll fall asleep. You'll put me in a deep state of unconsciousness and I'll be able to see things. Even if I won't remember anything afterwards, those things will help me feel better. I once helped with a hypnosis show in theatre. The hypnotizer counted, gave light touches, and made strange gestures and the people on stage fell asleep and did everything he told them to do. They acted like robots, like they had lost control."

Of course he was nervous, the poor guy!

I would have been nervous, too, if I found myself in front of a stranger who could transform me into a robot and take away my autonomy. Even though he had a good reputation and was recommended by a friend.

"Adrian, nothing could be farther from the truth," I told him. "Let me tell you what hypnosis really is." I explained to him that what he had just described to me was science fiction.

"So I won't lose control?" he asked me.

"Absolutely not. Not even for a moment," I told him. "That which we call hypnosis should more accurately be called auto-hypnosis. The professional serves to facilitate the process, and he guides the person along the experience, but only if the subject permits him to do so. It's a two-person job. Hypnosis serves to help people understand sensations, experiences, and memories, but it cannot force them to do so. The subject always has control. He can refuse to respond to questions, or do exactly the opposite of what is asked of him. He can even leave the hypnotic state, if he desires.

"If it weren't like this," I continued, "what would happen to you if I suddenly died? Would you remain there in a hypnotic state forever?" I joked. "Absolutely not. If I stopped talking to you while you were in a hypnotic state, the worst thing that could happen is you might fall asleep and then wake up a few minutes later. Or, you would simply think 'What is happening to this guy?' and you would leave the hypnotic state, opening your eyes on your own," I explained clearly, just as I do with everyone at the beginning of a session.

Thanks to modern neuroimaging techniques, in the past fifteen years there have been numerous studies on the efficacy of hypnosis and the changes it produces in the relevant areas of the brain. One study from 2009 (McGeown, et al.) demonstrated that during a meditation or hypnotic state, activity in the part of the brain called the "default mode network" is reduced. This network includes areas of the brain that are active when a person is not involved in any specific cognitive activity. Both the frontal and subcortical structures of the brain are in a relaxed state. Thus, a reduction in brain activity in these areas indicates a change in attention, directed by the instructions of the therapist. The study demonstrated that hypnosis is not a passive process in which one person gives information and the other receives it. Contrarily, it is a constructive process in which the involved person actively listens to the words of the professional and constructs his or her own ideas, sensations, and perceptions.

"So, I won't fall asleep?" Adrian asked.

"I sure hope not," I responded, "Otherwise it would be useless."

The induction of a hypnotic state and the work that can take place during this mental state produce results only if the conscious part of the brain remains present and in an operative state. Areas of consciousness in the cerebral cortex that are normally not active in a waking state are activated during a hypnotic state. It's a state in which the conscious and the subconscious mind can work together, and often produce results that therapy done with the conscious mind alone could not produce. This is precisely how the brain is able to rework sensations and perceptions from the deep subconscious in a conscious state, therefore putting things in the correct perspective, reconstituting equilibrium, and modifying false memories or non-current memories. Just as if it were a computer program, the hypnotic state gives the brain access to the hard drive of the subconscious, opens a "memory file," changes it, and then saves it again. This file is now ready to be used in a more functional way because it contains updated information.

I don't want to compare the divine beauty of our brain and our *psyche* to a man-made machine. But it is also true that the comparison is apt and that computers were created in our image. And just as a computer works better and more reliably with a correct and updated file, our mind, too, becomes more serene and balanced when a memory, either traumatic or not, is reworked and put in the correct perspective. And that's what happened, as we will see, with Adrian.

"So if I don't relax it won't work," replied Adrian, with a sense of frustration and disappointment. "As you can see Mr. Raco, I am not at all relaxed right now."

"The word hypnosis derives from the ancient Greek *hypnos*, which means 'sleep,'" I explained to him, "but people who are hypnotized are anything but asleep. Even if it seems to an outside observer that the person is asleep, in reality they find themselves in a hyper-conscious state, in which the brain is relaxed but at the same time extremely active.

"If you'll let me," I continued, "during the session we will use an EEG (electroencephalogram) machine, the latest BCI (brain computer interface) that will allow us to measure your cerebral activity. That way I'll be able to know how deep under you are at every moment. This will help me to better guide you and make your experience the best possible. As you'll see in the registration at the end of your session, the predominant cerebral waves will be *Alfa* waves, which come from a relaxed state in which the brain continues to be attentive and alert.

"It is precisely the coexistence of these two states, the state of consciousness and the emergence of the subconscious, which produces the best results," I explained to him. "If we used anesthesia or made you unconscious with medication, then the *Delta* waves of a cerebral coma would be dominant and you wouldn't remember anything. Therefore the conscious part of your brain would not be able to process information or gain any benefit from it," I told him.

However, as we will see later on in this book, during some past life regressions, even *Delta* waves have appeared in circumstances that I can testify are incredible.

Many neuroimaging studies performed with MRI and other techniques have demonstrated that hypnosis can produce changes at a cerebral level which sometimes seem to be at the base of therapeutic improvement. Can we say the same thing about past life regressions?

They certainly involve a hypnotic technique. But while it seems obvious that past memories of our current life reside in parts of our brains, even if they are hidden, where do memories of a past life come from?

Are we talking about Jung's collective unconscious?

Are they cellular memories that have traveled with us since the dawn of time?

If I could formulate a satisfying empirical scientific response, I would have solved humanity's greatest mystery. I might be even more famous than Leonardo or Galileo. But I don't think that this can be my objective, or that of any other man, because the impossibility of finding an answer to this question resides in the nature of man.

"It is a common illusion to believe that what we know today is all we ever can know. Nothing is more vulnerable and ephemeral than scientific theories, which are mere tools and not everlasting truths." Carl Gustav Jung

We humans and our science are extremely presumptuous. We act as if we can explain every phenomenon based on empirical demonstrations, on the observation of facts and experience. Thus science stops here in front of the insuperable limits of our five senses and the instruments, which are also our creation, that seek to amplify them. Doesn't that seem like an enormous limitation?

Now think of an earthworm. Think of a worm that lives underground, equipped only with rudimentary photoelectric cells that can determine dark from light. He is provided with only one sense, touch, which allows him to distinguish material in front of him and perceive the vibrations that come from the outside world, alerting him to danger. Like, for example, an approaching mole. Who are we to an earthworm? A scientific earthworm would say that we humans do not exist. When we walk on the earth above him, he would empirically observe only the results of an earthquake, but not our existence. Vice versa, the universe of the earthworm is extremely limited from our point of view, just as our universe and our desire to explain everything would be if looked at from the point of view of any being equipped with more than five senses. We would be to that being what the earthworm is to us.

So even our empirical science must still include ignorance and presumption. I get angry with myself when I think about my skepticism. Despite the fact that I have dedicated myself to years of past life regression therapy, gathering statistical proof and incredible testimonies about the existence of a much more vast reality than the material one, I continue to maintain a human and stubborn scientific and empirical attitude. The rational left part of my limited human brain does not want to admit anything it cannot measure, to the detriment of the facts themselves, which are still facts even if sometimes they are not demonstrable.

"One can understand and explain only when one has brought intuitions down to the safe basis of real knowledge of the facts and their logical connections. An honest investigator will have to admit that this is not possible in certain cases, but it would be dishonest of him to dismiss them on that account. Even a scientist is a human being, and it is quite natural that he, like others, hates the things he cannot explain and thus falls victim to the common illusion that what we know today represents the highest summit of knowledge." Carl Gustav Jung

As a man of science, I can perfectly understand how hypnosis and past life regressions have always been met with resistance from the scientific, academic, and institutional world. But a more Aristotelian view of reality could allow us to infer that sometimes the mere existence of a fact explains itself.

Human science is limited, so we have to accept our limits. Even if theoretically we are able to go back to the origin of the universe, the *Big Bang*, we cannot explain what produced it.

Theoretical physicists know very well that our two most important theories, Einstein's general relativity and quantum mechanics, are incompatible at a fundamental level. Modern physics travels on two parallel lines and even today is unable to formulate a theory that is capable of describing all observable phenomena.

But let's abide by human limits and return to our scientific desire to explain all observable phenomena, including regressions and past lives.

Dr. Daniel Amen, an illustrious American physician, double board-certified psychiatrist, multiple award-winning author of scientific books and publications, has dedicated himself for years to studying the brain using SPECT, Single-Photon Emission Computerized Tomography, a neuroimaging technique which is extremely new compared to others because it permits us to observe the brain in 3D. Among the over one hundred thousand SPECT scans done by Dr. Amen to examine and document the cerebral states of thousands of patients, one of them was performed on a patient who was under a past-life regression. The results were incredible: the brain was literally "illuminated" with new neural areas. Dense areas of memory that apparently didn't belong to the patient's current life, but to a past life. I showed the image of that SPECT scan to Adrian, who appeared worn out by all my explanations but definitely more relaxed. His face lost its reddish color and his body gave off fewer signals of nervousness. He had been a hard nut to crack, as I had found someone who was even more empirical and skeptical than I had been years earlier. But I was happy. He had given me the opportunity to remember that my own rational human brain is not omnipotent. I had done it! Adrian's nervousness had disappeared.

"Do horror movies scare you?" I asked him.

"Not particularly," he answered. "I'm not interested in them. But now that I'm thinking about it, every time I see a skull, I am overcome with a sense of anguish. I don't know why. I'm not afraid, but they make me terribly uncomfortable. They give me anxiety and I really can't understand why."

In that moment I didn't pay much attention to his issue. I thought it was just a normal fear of death. It's a fear that punctually disappears after a regression, when the person realizes that no one truly dies. After all, who likes skulls? They have always been an archetype dense with negative meanings.

He was really a hard nut to crack, I thought.

I always ask this question about horror films because it provides an immediate indication of how deep the person in front of me would be able to go. There is a very high correlation between the identification that a horror film produces and the capacity to enter into a hypnotic state.

And Adrian didn't have it.

"Fantastic," I thought sarcastically. A hyper-rational mind with little ability to identify, the worst type of subject for a hypnotic session. It was a challenge, so I had to put all of my abilities into play.

Today this type of situation wouldn't worry me at all. I have much more experience now and, as I said before, for some time I have been using, subject to the approval of the interested party, an EEG machine that registers cerebral activity during the session. Software on my computer continuously receives the data coming from the brain and shows the predominant cerebral waves as well as their level of attention and relaxation.

I can know what type of experience my client is having at every moment and how deep under they are. All of this obviously improves the quality of the experience for both of us: the client can have a much more profound and engaging experience, and I can guide them in the most appropriate manner at every moment.

But that day with Adrian, no apparatus would have been of help. The next step would be to establish a non-critical relationship with the methodology, which would be essential for its success. Because as I will never tire of saying, hypnosis is a two-person job. Without cooperation between the professional and the subject it is impossible to establish any type of communication between the conscious and the subconscious.

Some people think that during the hypnotic state they will tell all the secrets they have stored safe and deep in the back of their mind.

"Hypnosis is not a truth serum," I explained to Adrian. "During hypnosis you will always maintain control and you will decide what you want to tell me and what you don't. If you don't want to tell me something, I assure you that you won't tell me. If I were to ask you about something that you don't want to share, you would simply tell me that it's none of my business. No one will ever obligate you in any way to reveal information that your mind considers personal. During the hypnotic state the subject is even able to lie. I'm obviously not telling you that you'll do that, because it wouldn't make any sense; I just want to reassure you that you will have control the entire time."

Adrian clearly appeared more relaxed and interested. His posture and his expression reflected that change in attitude. Now he was sitting on the edge of his seat, his chest thrust towards me. He looked me directly in the eyes and lost all trace of a flushed face. His small eyes lit up and demonstrated a growing interest and above all, from my point of view, a growing desire to live this new experience. He was about to express the last of his fears.

"Do you think I'll be able to be hypnotized?" he asked me. "I'm so rational."

"Don't worry. If you trust me, and we work together, that's something for me to worry about," I responded.

To the great joy of my ego, I can say that my success rate is very high, even with extremely rational subjects such as Adrian.

"Practically everyone can be hypnotized," I reassured him. "The capabilities of a professional come from experience and from his ability to find the correct induction methodology for each person. With these parameters success is practically guaranteed. You just have to let yourself go to my instructions. Our job now is to gather information, not analyze it. We'll have all the time in the world, after the session, to do so and to come to conclusions."

It's also useful to remember that hypnosis is just an instrument and it does not constitute a therapy in and of itself. The benefits are reached through synergic communication between the conscious and subconscious mind that the hypnotic technique can facilitate; but the effect is obviously also attributed to the experience and the training of the professional who is practicing it. If I didn't specify that, I would betray my Jungian approach and my four years and over 350 sessions of psychoanalysis as a patient, which are an integral part of my training and of my method. Regarding the result of a past life regression, I can say that the soul is the true protagonist of any interior work.

Sometimes, the success of the hypnotic technique can be really astonishing, even for those who practice it. I remember a past life regression that I had the privilege and good fortune to conduct during an international congress; in that seminar over sixty percent of the 200 or so participants were able to remember a past life. And it was a group regression, in which one doesn't have the ability to personalize the induction technique nor to singularly guide the person through the experience.

"Anyone can reach a hypnotic state. Sometimes it's just a matter of practice." I continued, "It is a state in which we find ourselves more and more each day, maybe without even realizing it. When we read a book, even if absorbed in the story, we know perfectly well what is happening around us, so we find ourselves in a hypnotic state. When we drive a car and simultaneously talk on the phone (on speakerphone, don't forget!), we find ourselves in a hypnotic state. When we cook and talk with our family or friends, we find ourselves in a hypnotic state. We enter and leave a hypnotic state many times a day, and we do it so well that we don't even realize it anymore. Even meditation is essentially an auto-hypnotic state. And, as we have seen, neuroimaging techniques demonstrate this."

"So what is the difference between hypnosis and meditation?" Adrian then asked me.

"At a cerebral level there is no difference between states. The difference is purely technical. In meditation, people have to produce in themselves that specific state of consciousness, and they can do it in a variety of ways, using breathing, relaxation, focalization, concentration, mindfulness, etc. Normally it requires a fair amount of effort, sometimes even years of practice, because it is difficult to stop the automatic and continual functioning of our brain. During a session of hypnosis the state is induced by the therapist, and this normally happens within a few minutes, sometimes even within a few seconds. Another difference is that the meditation state normally lasts only a few seconds, or minutes when the person has been practicing a long time. With hypnosis the trance state can be maintained for much longer, permitting the subject to understand many more things.

And, above all, the subject can be guided during the experience, something that is not possible with meditation, where the role of a guide is developed by the conscious part of the brain which more often than not is anything but cooperative."

The comparison with meditation had, without a doubt, rendered the work complete. Adrian was now much more relaxed, so much so that he smiled at me. He seemed like a different person than the man who entered my office.

Milton Erickson, one of the great fathers of hypnosis whose theories and methodologies contributed to my training as a graduate student, sustained that sometimes hypnotic inductions can be very similar to a normal conversation, which often uses metaphors and a poetic and persuasive language. According to Erickson, one can suggest solutions to the subconscious using words, circumventing the resistance and repression that the conscious mind uses to resist change.

This was exactly what Adrian and I had done during the first part of this session. I couldn't help it, and I would probably never have a normal conversation again, with anybody. I would always be a hypnotizer, I thought sarcastically.

In any case, that conversation had a positive effect on Adrian, who by now was ready. So I invited him to lie down on the *chaise longue* that I use for regression, and I proceeded with the more formal induction technique, which led him within a few minutes into a profound trance.

"I see little feet," Adrian began. "They are clean. They look like the feet of a child. I am walking in the grass and it's a nice day, not too hot or too cold. I'm in a field."

"They aren't children's feet… I'm a woman!" Adrian stated with surprise.

"What's your name?" I asked him. Or rather, her.

"My name is Lucille." She answered me instantaneously, without a moment of hesitation. And he laughed.

Adrian himself realized in that moment that there was no doubt – that information was not a product of his conscious brain.

"How old are you?" I asked.

"I am about thirty."

"Where are you?"

"In France, the south of France."

"What year is it?"

"It's 1920."

"How are you dressed?"

"I'm wearing a long dress, white and blue. It almost reaches my feet. I also have a petticoat, I think. I am wearing a cloth belt that's a darker color, almost black. I have blonde hair and I wear it gathered behind my head."

"Do you live near there?" I asked.

"Yes, I can see my house. It's a simple house, made of wood. There is also a mustached man with a wagon. He's funny. He is wearing light brown baggy pants that reach his knees, a white shirt, and a dark gilet. He seems from a long time ago."

"It is a long time ago! It's 1920!" I added, knowing that the conscious and rational part of his brain was trying to analyze and intervene to re-take control.

"On the wooden steps that lead to my house there is a child. He has curly hair, and he's beautiful. He is five years old and his name is Augustin. He's my son!"

A few tears fell down Adrian's face. They were tears of joy, Lucille's tears.

But they were also Adrian's tears, because when I asked him if little Augustin was someone who his soul recognized in his present life, he responded quickly:

"It's my young son, Ivan!" and the tears became true, freeing, tears of joy.

This is a normal occurrence. One of our biggest fears does not lie in death in and of itself, but in the idea of having to abandon the people we love the most. Knowing that it is only a "see you later," that our loved ones do not abandon us but travel with us during many lives, makes us feel better and frees our souls from the earthly binds that constrain them. And Adrian's face in that moment reflected a state of immense happiness.

"What do you do for work? How do you occupy your days?" I asked when I saw that he had recovered.

"I go to the river to do the laundry. I take care of Augustin and the animals. We have hens and horses. I take care of the house."

I then took him to a later moment in Lucille's existence and we both discovered, even if I did not push for it, that it was the moment of her death.

"I am in another house, on a bed. I can't breathe," he began. He became red in the face. In a moment, the physical sensation he was feeling finished and he returned to breathing normally.

"I am about seventy years old. I am dying of something involving the lungs, because I can't breathe."

He continued, "There is a man with a beard in the room. Maybe it's a hospital, because he certainly seems to be a doctor. There is also a woman who is holding my hand, a dear friend. In my real life I don't know her, but I can feel that Lucille really loves her. She was my dearest friend. I don't want to die, it's very sad. Her friendship and her presence helped me in every way during life. Augustin had gone to war, in the Second World War. He didn't come back." He began to cry again, and then experienced death.

"What does it feel like to die? What is the sensation?" I asked him. Then I added, "If you had to describe it to a human being, how would you explain it?"

It's a good time to specify this, because the majority of people who have done a regression under my guidance have been incapable of describing otherworldly sensations, labeling them more often than not as sensations that they had never felt before, ones whose profundity and strength fall outside human consciousness. And the fact that everyone describes the same type of experience is a statistical proof, even for a rational and stubborn person such as myself.

"I'm good. Very good. I am hovering over my body. I feel at peace, and I am not suffering anymore."

"So death, that scares us all so much, is in reality a happy experience?" I asked.

"Yes. I'm great. I am only sad because I won't see Augustin anymore."

With experience, I can say that this type of sensation is very common. It's almost absurd to think that Adrian, who had recognized in little Augustin his son Ivan, who lives with him and who he sees every day, felt such strong feelings of sadness. It's more proof that in that moment he was suffering in Lucille's shoes.

Frequently in the moments immediately after death we remain attached to the existence that we are leaving. Even if we already find ourselves in celestial form, we continue to experience the sensations of that life, and we say goodbye to the people we have loved. That's how it was for Adrian; in Lucille's shoes he was saying goodbye to his Augustin, even if an hour later Adrian would have met Augustin's soul in his son Ivan and could hug him again.

"That which one life takes from us, another gives it back."

Suffering is never an end in itself. The universe always has good motives, even if things sometimes seem cruel or useless.

"I am going higher and higher up," Adrian said. "I can see the house from on high. It wasn't a hospital, it was my friend's house. Now I know.

"There is a presence near me. It is very luminous. It's a strong light, but it isn't bothersome. It's as if it passes through me. I feel good. It is hugging me and smiling. It doesn't have legs or a face. But I know it's her, it's my mother, Lucille's mom. She is telling me not to be afraid, to be calm because soon I will see Augustin again."

And that's exactly how it was, because Ivan was waiting for him at home and soon they would see each other again.

Adrian woke up, coming back to a normal state of consciousness. And even if I was happy that he was able to let himself go, understand and experience the immortality of the soul, and enjoy the fact that he and his son Ivan have known each other forever, something told me that things weren't going to end there.

There were too many unfinished questions that this existence couldn't explain. Normally the first life that our soul permits us to remember is an important and meaningful life.

Was it an important life for Adrian?

Without a doubt he understood that his son Ivan was the most important person in his current life. But my experience told me that there was still a missing piece of the puzzle. I couldn't understand how Adrian's experience would help him with his symptoms of depression. I asked him if he wanted to come back for another session. He told me yes and we made another appointment.

The next week when Adrian came back to my office, he was wearing another white shirt and I noticed that he wasn't sweaty at all. He said hello to me with a huge and radiant smile. I asked him how it was going and he said he hadn't had any panic attacks that week and that he felt more serene; he had been skeptical, but our session was having positive effects.

I asked him then to make himself comfortable on the couch and I proceeded with the induction technique. This time was much easier and faster. Hypnosis is an exercise of the mind. The more you do it, the simpler it becomes. And it is precisely for this reason that I always teach auto-hypnosis techniques to the people who do multiple sessions with me, in case they have trouble falling asleep or simply as a meditation instrument.

Instead of bringing him to a past life, this time I decided to regress him to his childhood. It is a technique that I used often, as we will see later on in this book.

"I am in a dimly lit room," Adrian began. "I'm afraid."

His voice had already become higher and shriller. The tones and expressions were effectively that of a child. This was a sign that the hypnotic trance was deep enough.

"How old are you?" I asked him.

"I am eight years old."

"Is it night?" I asked him.

"No. It's day. But the blinds are lowered. Only a little light comes in. I want to get out of here!"

He seemed to be getting more and more anxious and worried.

"Are you at your house? Where are you?"

"I am at my neighbor's house, in the garage. He's helping me fix my bike."

"Is there someone with you?"

"No. No one is here now. He told me to wait here."

"Who told you to wait there?"

"My neighbor. His wife and his daughter are at home, in the living room. He always tells me to wait there for him. In front of me in the garage is a poster with a skull. It scares me."

"Why do you have to wait there for him?" I asked, curious but at the same time worried. I feared I knew how this story was going to end.

"He always tells me to wait. When he comes back I have to have my pants lowered, otherwise he gets mad."

"Why?" I asked, knowing exactly what the response was going to be.

"Because he wants to touch me."

"Where?"

"Down there. I don't want it. It scares me, and it disgusts me. But if I don't let him do it he will tell my parents. He will say it was me who lowered my paints. I want him to stop."

Adrian began to cry, just as an eight-year-old child would have.

"I want you now to imagine that your neighbor is in the garage in front of you." I told him, "He is looking at you but he can't talk, he can't yell, he can't touch you, he can't laugh at you, he can't hit you, he can't threaten you, he can't do anything besides listen to you without replying. Can you imagine him?" I asked.

"Yes," Adrian replied.

"I want you now to talk directly to him and tell him what you think and how his behavior makes you feel. I want you to make him understand the feelings you have. He has to realize the consequences that his actions had on you."

This technique of revivification is very effective and is also used to treat post-traumatic stress disorder because it permits the conscious part of the brain to rework forgotten memories in the subconscious and repair traumatic injuries.

"You disgust me. I hate you. You are a disgusting pig," yelled Adrian, crying. And he continued to yell at his neighbor, ordering him to stop, emptying his soul of the anger, the hate, and the rancor that he had had since he was a child. He said everything he hadn't had the courage to say when he was little. He yelled and cried until he reached an apparent state of calm.

I then brought Adrian to a pleasant memory from his childhood. He saw himself again at his fourth birthday party, surrounded by family that loved him, in an atmosphere of great joy and serenity. I always proceed in this manner before waking someone up and bringing them back to a state of normal consciousness after they relived very traumatic events. The subconscious work has already been done and this trip constitutes a more pleasant return to the present.

Adrian was shocked and pleasantly affected by the experience. He told me that up until a few minutes before he didn't remember anything about those episodes. He must have completely removed them from his memory to continue living normally, I thought. He was unable to live with the interior malaise that those things provoked in him. It was a totally normal and understandable reaction. In the presence of a traumatic event that causes us deep pain, one that we cannot confront in any way, our brain enacts a very efficient survival strategy: it removes the memory and hides it in the subconscious. This permits us to carry on, to survive the pain. Unfortunately the memory remains present and until it is processed in a way that reestablishes equilibrium, it can cause important psychological and physical problems, just like what happened in Adrian's case.

A few months later I had the opportunity to see Adrian again. He told me his symptoms of anxiety and depression had totally disappeared, and that he had been sleeping normally again and could dedicate himself to activities that interested him. He told me he felt happier and more sure of himself, now the master of his own life. Now he doesn't have any problems finding himself alone with his children nor with children in general. He even organized a birthday party for Ivan. He told me that he finalized his separation from his wife and was now living alone. He is very happy that his two children, Ivan and his older brother, spend weekends at his house.

Even his relationship with his father had completely changed after the regression. He realized he had always blamed his father, who wasn't aware of what happened, and who at that time wasn't able to protect him from his neighbor.

"And I want you to choose some time in the past when you were a very, very little girl. And my voice will go with you. And my voice will change into that of your parents, your neighbors, your friends, your schoolmates, your playmates, your teachers. And I want you to find yourself sitting in the school room, a little girl feeling happy about something, something that happened a long time ago, that you forgot a long time ago."
Milton H. Erickson

PROBLEMS AND MEMORIES

When Marta came back to see me, after her first regression in which she saw herself as a bear in the forest, her face was more luminous and her expression was even sweeter. Something had changed in that woman who had given off a powerful energy since the first time I saw her. Her slender stature and small frame, the grace of her movements, and her refined feminine taste in clothing emphasized the power emanating from her gaze. She had hypnotic eyes, capable of transmitting a steadfastness and serenity, and full of unconditional love. It was truly a pleasure seeing her for another session.

She wore her hair bobbed, short and blonde, and her beauty didn't need makeup to be appreciated. The serenity of her gaze attracted attention, making everything else fall to second place.

It was a spring day, one of those days in which the little tables outside restaurants and cafés on the Rambla de Catalunya in Barcelona fill up with people and happiness. Marta was dressed in an emerald green silk dress that went down to just above her knee, with a small golden belt positioned just under her breast. She looked like she came out of a 1950s *Vogue* cover, wearing an Audrey Hepburn-style dress that emphasized Marta's sweet, loving, extremely pure attitude. She called me "Maestro" when she spoke to me, and she spoke little. She was never a chatty woman, but every one of her words sounded full of significance, important. She was seated in front of me and I was no longer sure who was the hypnotizer and the hypnotized, who was the student and the maestro.

I consider this profession a mission, but undeniably it is a mission that gives me great privileges. First and foremost being the possibility to interact with many people, marvelous souls, earthly angels who, sometimes, as was the case with Marta, didn't even suspect that they were such.

That day I had in front of me a blonde and modern Audrey Hepburn. "Who knows," I thought to myself, "Maybe Marta really is the reincarnation that eternal actress' soul." Soon we would find out. I smiled to myself, at that funny thought.

It was a highly improbable eventuality, practically impossible. I know perfectly well, thanks to hundreds of regressions that I've conducted on other patients, that the probability of having been a famous person in a past life is practically zero.

The number of sessions continues to grow even as I write this book, heightening my gratitude towards the universe that put me on the correct path. I still remember my first regression with Brian nine years ago and the words of my celestial masters: you have to dedicate yourself to helping others, they told me. That experience brought me to the conclusion that I would dedicate a part of my time to regressions, and I would do so without financial gain. This decision permitted people to come to me who would not have otherwise had the resources. And it obviously influenced the number of people that I had the luck and the capacity to regress. Today I am even more sure that it was the right decision and that the universe knew how to compensate me with the practice, and I was able to acquire valuable experience in a relatively short time.

And so, even with many regressions in my pocket, I only came upon a famous person once. I will describe that experience in greater detail in a following chapter. My left brain, the rational and skeptical part, gets great satisfaction out of the fact that I have hardly met a famous person in a past life at all, because it thinks a regression to an anonymous person from long ago must be more truthful. It confirms to me that we're dealing with genuine experiences; if it had anything to do with imagination my sessions would probably be filled with the souls of Napoleon, Joan of Arc, and Marilyn Monroe. Statistics, thanks to the large number of regressions, gave me a way to confirm that hypnosis reawakens memories. I have had the fortune of playing spectator to hundreds of normal and common experiences, stories that were apparently simple but, at the same time, moving in their humanity.

I decided that day to use our session to regress Marta to episodes from her childhood, given that I didn't expect any bad surprises, judging by the serenity emanating from the girl. I invited her to lay down on the couch, beginning my induction into the hypnotic relaxed state.

"I'm in the bedroom with my sister," Marta began.

"How old are you?" I asked.

"Two years old," she said. "How strange, I had completely forgotten this room, because the following year we changed houses. It's all blue. My sister and I had fun here. We played and jumped on the bed, she on hers and I on mine. I like it so much..."

"Oh no!" continued Marta. "While jumping I fell to the ground. I hit my face on the corner of the dresser. It really hurt!"

"Are you really feeling pain?" I asked her.

I always do this when I see my client's expression changes as they lay there with their eyes closed. I don't want them to experience actual feelings of pain.

"Yes. The front of my head hurts" she responded.

Thanks to an effective hypnotic suggestion that got rid of all the pain, I made it so that Marta's face wasn't red anymore and her expression became relaxed.

"I cut my forehead. I don't feel any more pain but I know they brought me to the hospital, because they had to give me ten or so external stitches and even more internal ones. They will become infected and the scar will remain forever."

The session continued with other moments from her childhood and adolescence without any striking or particularly unusual events. The surprise for me arrived that same evening, when I received Marta's text message, which said this:

I returned to the apartment which I rented for my stay, had an early dinner, then I sat on my couch to write my partner and update him on the day. Suddenly the lights went out. Other than the light in the living room none of the appliances were working, nothing. I immediately called the landlord, because the circuit breaker seemed to be blocked, and he promised me that he would immediately call a trusted electrician. Then I remembered that I would have to look out the window to see if the technician had arrived, because without electricity the buzzer wouldn't work. I had to look out. From the fifth floor! For me, an impossible task. Just a few meters is enough to terrorize me, normally. But I felt strangely strong after the hypnosis. Ready to try. It seemed as if destiny was giving me the opportunity to try. Normally I would never have been able to go near the window, but this evening I inched closer and closer. And, to my immense surprise, I was able to see, immediately and without panic, the sidewalk below. Five floors down!

It's always magic to participate in the amazing results of this incredible technique. Seeing problems or phobias disappear in a few hours that could have affected my client's entire life, like Marta's fear of heights, reminds me daily how lucky I am to dedicate my time to something so marvelous.

I obviously remained in contact with Marta, who recently told me that she continued to challenge herself with heights and doesn't have problems with it anymore. She's even thinking of going paragliding, she said. That would have been absolutely impossible for her before that hypnosis experience.

Another woman, whom I will call Carla to maintain her privacy, had a similar story. In her story, as we will see, the root of the problem would be found by going further back in time than with Marta. Carla was a thin girl who wasn't very tall, with curly long blonde hair and a beautiful smile. When I met her for the first time I realized she was very shy, but that her radiant smile was worth a thousand words. One could sense that she was a positive person just by looking into her shiny, big green eyes. Dressed in a hippie-chic style, for all I knew she could have just come out of a '60s Volkswagen van that had just arrived at a rock concert. She was wearing a cream-colored shirt coupled with a light brown leather vest, and tucked into her shirt was a pair of metal sunglasses, round, which I later discovered were very fashionable. Bell-bottom jeans and a satchel purse completed the look. It was clear that for her this outfit was totally natural and had nothing to do with fads. She said she was happy to come and see me and that she couldn't wait to have what she herself termed "an incredible experience." She had read about hypnosis and regressions but she struggled to believe that what she was about to experience could really happen.

She was a challenge for me, I thought. It's difficult to respond to such high expectations, and a good professional also needs to bring people back down to earth. "The trance is an experience that happens daily and naturally," Milton Erickson, the father of modern hypnosis, reminds us. Even if many people have high expectations, the hypnotic trance is not comparable to a 3D film, a hallucination, or a lucid dream.

As always, I put her at ease and asked her to tell me about her life, and if there were special motives that pushed her in this direction. She explained to me that she had travelled a lot and she had just finished a course in *Reiki* (an ancient Japanese discipline that focuses on harmonizing the energy in the body) that made her understand the importance of the human energy field and reflect on how our energy can outlive our bodies. Her curiosity about regressions and past lives came from this. If energy existed even outside the body, she said to me, then it would be able to endure even after death. She told me that she had come mostly out of curiosity, but that she also had a practical problem that plagued her: she had just changed jobs and her new job required frequent travel. Unfortunately Carla had not been able to drive for over four years. She told me that when she got in the car and drove over 25 mph, an unthinkably slow speed outside of the city, she got strong anxiety, had difficulty breathing, and got heart palpitations. I asked her if that problem had begun after some concrete event in her life, in which case I would recommend a good psychiatrist or clinical psychologist. She told me that it all started randomly after returning from a trip to Northern Europe. I asked her to tell me in detail about the experience, but there didn't seem to be any correlation between the trip and the onset of the symptoms that made it difficult for her to drive.

The whole thing was getting very interesting, from my point of view. My sixth sense said the explanation of her phobia might have an origin further back in time. And my sixth sense wasn't wrong.

I asked her to lie down on the couch and I turned on the background music. Then I began the progressive relaxation hypnotic technique.

Carla suddenly began to move, without saying a word or making any sound. She lost her radiant expression and her face seemed profoundly worried. Her cheeks reddened as she began to twitch.

"What's happening?" I asked her.

"They are following me," she said.

"Who?"

"Knights, they're right behind me. They are wearing armor. I'm wearing it too, and it seems like I have a heavy sword at my side, I can't see very well from inside the helmet. I'm escaping, but my horse isn't fast enough. They will catch up to me soon."

"Where are you?"

"I'm in a field. It seems like a clearing surrounded by forest. I can see my city. I am fighting to save it."

"What city are we talking about?' I asked her.

"It's a little city in Belgium, northwest of Brussels."

"What is your name," I asked, thinking she was a man in that life.

"Mary Ann," Carla responded.

"You're a woman?" I said, extremely surprised.

"Yes, I'm a woman. I dressed up as a man and I'm wearing a knight's armor."

"Why are they following you?"

"We are fighting. They invaded our city and they killed the man that I loved. His name was John. I loved him so dearly and they killed him. He was also trying to defend our city from invaders, so I decided to take his place and fight, to avenge his death."

"What year is it?" I asked her.

"1584," Carla said.

She responded immediately and without hesitation. I still haven't gotten used to it, even after many regressions, how the historic details of past lives appear to someone in a regression in an immediate and precise way. They always respond to me instantly and without a shadow of a doubt. The skeptical and rational part of my brain is profoundly surprised every time: they literally don't have time to think, let alone invent.

"They've almost reached me," Carla said. "They are quickly coming up behind me. They wounded my horse and he's fallen over. I get thrown in the air, I'm flying. I fall to the ground, and I feel that I'm dying."

"How did it happen?" I asked.

"I'm crashing against a sharp rock. I'm dead. I have left my body and I can see the scene from above. There are five enemy knights kneeling around me, checking to make sure that I'm really dead. They don't even take off my armor. They don't care to find out who I am, because they would never imagine they had killed John's woman in a suit of armor. But I don't care anymore, I'm leaving the life of Mary Ann. I feel that I now understand how important my independence as a woman is. In that lifetime, I didn't stand on the sidelines to watch. I reacted, I was courageous. I feel that this courage belongs to me now, in Carla's life. I feel strong and free."

After the session Carla seemed even more serene and radiant than before. I could tell that she felt optimistic and newly sure of herself. She was ready to confront any work challenge that life was preparing for her; just like Mary Ann, no obstacle could stand in her way. She was a courageous woman, and she always knew it. But the real surprise arrived a few days later, when I received a text message from Carla. She emotionally thanked me because after over four years she was finally able to drive on the highway again. Reliving her fall from Mary Ann's horse had finally liberated Carla from that subconscious memory that impeded her from getting around as she liked. She was truly, and newly, free.

It's not always necessary to undergo a regression to free ourselves from a past life memory that traps us in bad situations or a present life malaise. Our past lives can manifest themselves in our subconscious or in our conscious mind even during dreams and daily experiences, like déjà vu. Albert, a forty-year-old man who lives in Milan and became a dear friend of mine, had an experience that confirmed this. Albert has always been passionate about Hungary, without an apparent reason. He visited the country numerous times and once he even served as my guide, permitting me to learn about the beauty of *art nouveau* and the customs of the marvelous city of Budapest in detail.

My experience is very simple - Albert told me. - *I was coming back one late afternoon from an outing in Southern Hungary that was organized by a dear Hungarian friend. We had gone to Szeged, his native city, to see his parents. When we returned to the city my friend decided to stop at his home. I was happy about our excursion and the nice sunny day, so I decided to dedicate the remainder of the day to exploring the eighth district of Budapest. Today, this is the quarter where the Romani (Gypsies) live, although close to the area, near Blaha Lujza square, there is a refined and beautiful hotel. I entered a dark street which was full of menacing faces.*

The residents of Budapest avoid that part of the city just as your brothers in New York stay away from the Bronx - Albert said to me, referring to my residence in the USA as a young man. -

I decided to go anyway, encouraged by the time of day. It was only six in the afternoon and splendidly sunny. The eighth district is also adjacent to the Corvin Negyed, the square next to the beautiful Museum of Applied Arts, the one with the huge majolica green roof. From there I began to walk, guided by an interior compass. I had taken a quick look at the district on the map, but I didn't study the streets in detail. I was struck by the public garden in the middle of Mattia square, named after the mythical and much loved medieval Magyar king, in an area of the city that was totally without greenery.

I continued in this way, guided by my intuition, and I arrived at Horvath Mihaly square. I looked at the beautiful school, constructed in the art nouveau style, and I noticed a house on the corner and an enormous yellow church. I continued to look around like a simple tourist.

Then, inexplicably, instead of turning left to go back to the city center, I told myself: No, I have to go right. I knew quite well that Baross Utca Street, in that direction, led to the cemetery, and that certainly wasn't my aim. I saw a house with two little pointed towers and a strange metallic front. It was telling me something, I felt like I already knew it. So I decided to keep going, and on the first street to the left I felt like I needed to keep going down that street. There was no reason to go down that anonymous little street, even if something was pushing me to go that way.

I had an irrational and groundless desire. I arrived at the end, and I was struck and fascinated by the little square that the street fed into, in which there was a music school, situated at a picturesque angle, and the area was closed off to automobiles. I kept going, taking myself farther from the center. I was strangely unafraid, even if I knew I had found myself in a less than reputable area of town. I turned right from the little square with the two schools. Suddenly at the next corner I was shocked to see a wooden crucifix in the middle of the street, right near a small and dilapidated house.

I had seen that crucifix before! But where? Where? Maybe during the mountain walks I took as a child? Where? In some book about art? I couldn't remember, yet I was sure I knew it. I knew it. I stood there for a minute in a state of shock, then I decided to keep going. A few meters after the crucifix I reached Mattia Square, the one with the public garden, and I saw in the corner a marvelous art nouveau building, a work of art from the beginning of the nineteenth century, with an old sign that said 'Magda Udvar' (Magda Department Store). The name Magda reminded me of a client of the practice where I work, and a strange sensation of familiarity came to me whenever I said her name, even though I hardly knew her.

I walked a few meters further in the square, crossing it diagonally, along the small street of the public garden that would bring me straight home.

Suddenly a violent sensation overcame me, strong and incredible. I looked at the house and saw a window! That bow window!

My heart started beating faster. Shivers ran through me. I trembled. I began to cry and I couldn't stop, even though there was no reason to be sad.

A voice inside me said: "you lived here. And your friend lived in the small house next door, to the left, on the other side of the street."

Even now when I'm telling this story, after years, I shiver.

I had to sit down on a bench and I remained there, almost catatonic, crying for a while. In the following days I felt the necessity to return there every day, as if I were doing a pilgrimage.

With the help of dreams and meditations I was able to, bit by bit, remember the events of those last years of the nineteenth century. I remembered the room with the bow window, the big window, the ample table, a huge wooden globe, a fireplace, and myself dressed in a white shirt with suspenders. I remembered that on that day in 1892 I was looking just out the window when Mark, my lover, an English diplomat stationed in Budapest, attempted to stab me in the back with an enormous knife. I know that we were homosexuals and we had a clandestine relationship but I didn't remember the details. I have always been afraid to find out more. Having read the books by Dr. Brian Weiss I obviously thought of you. I'm happy to finally be able to tell you this story. Albert concluded.

Albert is a homosexual in his present life as well. This experience helped him to understand many of the events in his current life, such as the end of his romance with his last companion and the sensation of fear and mistrust and the incessant fights that led him to end that relationship. Those feelings had nothing to do with Albert's actual partner, because they belonged to the past life in Budapest, but they negatively influenced their relationship. Today Albert and his ex-partner are friends and they finally care about each other, tied by an invisible thread that unites their souls forever, as with all soul mates. Having had access, even if just spontaneously, to the experience of that life, Albert today is ready to love again without fear and hesitation.

Albert's experience is not common for a few reasons: Firstly, that he was able to access, spontaneously and exhaustively, the happenings of a past life; second, that he was able to relive a past life in which he was homosexual, just as he is in his present life. During our many lifetimes, we are all usually given the opportunity to play many roles, as men and women, and to experience all the different aspects of the sentimental and sexual sphere. I will never forget the stupor, which eventually was quite fun, of a conservative woman, a member of the high society, who was over sixty years old, a mother of three children and grandmother of five: she came to me for a regression and she saw herself as a young man from ancient Rome, in love with his slave, with whom he had more or less clandestine sexual relations.

The story of another girl, whom I will call Sarah, also has some points in common with the other stories told thus far. Sarah was twenty-nine years old when she came to see me for the first time. She was a beautiful girl with long blonde hair. She had large, green eyes and pale skin. I thought that her skin and her shape would have made her perfect for makeup commercials. She had an angelic face that seemed to emanate positive energy.

A few years ago I would never have used this expression. My scientific and materialistic attitude would never have allowed me to even hypothesize that people could give off energy. I remember when Dr. Brian Weiss chose me for a regression out of over a thousand other people at one of his seminars. As soon as I got up on stage he told me that he had chosen me because I had a face that emanated a particular light. I was very flattered even if I didn't believe in those types of things back then. A year later, in the United States, I had the opportunity to speak with an established psychic medium who had participated in many scientific studies. I asked her to clarify the matter for me, and whether she too was able to see the lights that people emitted. She told me that we all can, that we are all connected, and that it's only a matter of learning to use our abilities. Even if back then it seemed silly, now I can tell you that it is absolutely possible. Thanks to experience, and having known many people deep down in their souls, I slowly began to perceive the light that each of us radiates. And I can confirm what that medium told me: we can all do it. It has to do with what we usually call intuition, a sixth sense that always accompanies us, whether we know it or not. It has to do with learning the language, recognizing the dynamics. But it is not difficult nor is it impossible. It is a language of the soul. If as a total skeptic I was able to do it, you can do it too.

Sarah's pale face and her energy were in stark contrast with her neo-punk clothes: black leggings with black leather military-style boots and a black heavy metal shirt. Anyone would have thought she was a rebel at first glance; this was the message of her look. After a few minutes of conversation I asked her to tell me about herself; I discovered that essentially she was a rebel, but her rebellion consisted in being a pacifist, animal lover, and vegan. We spoke about being vegan or vegetarian and the personal motivations behind this choice. I explained to her that I personally understood it: for years I hadn't drank any milk or eaten almost any milk products or cheeses. I am not uncompromising in this choice of mine, however. If I am invited to dinner at a friend's house I am not picky nor do I ask to change the menu. I also obviously don't proselytize because my choice is personal, a form of respect towards animals. In reality I am not against a meat-based diet in and of itself, as much as I am against the industrial and intensive raising of animals, where the animals live out existences full of suffering. Ancient societies, like the Native Americans, have always used animals for food, being part of the food chain, but they always did it without provoking unnecessary suffering. They were thankful and honored the sacrifice of the slaughtered creatures. For this reason I decided to limit my consumption of animal products as much as possible, allowing myself only the mozzarella on a piece of pizza or occasionally some sushi or fried fish. Sarah was much stricter than I was. I still have a lot to learn, I thought, seeing the extra dedication she had to a principle we essentially shared.

I asked her, as I always do, what pushed her to come see me.

"I've been suffering from anxiety for a few years now, but lately it's getting worse," Sarah responded. "Sometimes when I get panic attacks I can't catch my breath, and for me this is really serious because I've had asthma since I was about eight years old."

"I understand," I responded. "I can confirm that many people who suffer from anxiety attacks and agoraphobia experience the same unpleasant sensation. Anxiety is our physiological response to an external stimulus that the brain perceives as danger; sometimes it can be as simple as a daily situation that we don't want to confront. In the face of this 'danger' the brain produces a physiological response: the heart pumps blood faster and raises the heart rate, and the breathing rate also speeds up to bring more oxygen to the muscles. They are innate mechanisms that allow us to prepare our bodies to react or flee in the face of a threat, mechanisms that activate even if the danger is not real, merely perceived. Besides, the definition of 'danger' is totally subjective. For some people it could be something merely unexpected, and for others perhaps something that induces anxiety. During a panic attack, many people can even be afraid of suffocating and dying. This is impossible in a patient with normal pulmonary capacity, because the effect is exactly the opposite: raising the breathing rate introduces more air into the lungs. Obviously it's not the same for a person who suffers from asthma, in which the pulmonary capacity is compromised, so I perfectly understand your concerns, Sarah."

"First of all I will teach you some breathing exercises that will help you take control over your feelings of anxiety," I reassured Sarah again, who really seemed quite worried.

"They are mindfulness exercises, according to the technique developed by Jon Kabat-Zinn, the leading world expert of this discipline," I explained to her.

Kabat-Zinn defines mindfulness as *paying attention, on purpose, in the present moment, and non-judgmentally.* So mindfulness means paying voluntary attention to that which is happening inside our body and around us, instant after instant, and observing the experience for what it is without evaluating it or criticizing it. The practice of this discipline derives from Theravada Buddhism, one of the two main branches of Buddhism, well-known for 2,500 years in Southern and Southeast Asia, in particular Burma, Cambodia, Sri Lanka and Thailand, in both religious and secular environments. The use of mindfulness in Western medicine as a health technique is a relatively recent development, beginning in the 1970s in the United States by the same Kabat-Zinn as one of the first methodologies of stress reduction.

"I learned about this methodology during my training in Mindfulness-Based Cognitive Therapy, a therapy that uses meditation and mindfulness to prevent relapses of depression, and I assure you that it has had optimal results in the management of anxiety. You have to use it just as you begin to perceive you are entering a state of anxiety."

So I asked her to stay seated, close her eyes, and rest her hands on her knees, letting her arms fall comfortably down at her sides.

"Take three deep breaths," I told Sarah, and once she had finished the three breaths I said "Now begin to breathe normally through your nose. I would like you to pay attention to the air that enters and exits your nostrils. Now count mentally with me," I continued and, following the rhythm of her breathing, began counting out loud. "*One* breath in with the nose, *two* breath out with the nose, *three* inhale, *four* exhale, *five* inhale, *six* exhale, *seven* inhale, *eight* exhale, *nine* inhale, *ten* exhale," and I then continued counting backwards. "*Ten* inhale, *nine* exhale, *eight* inhale, *seven* exhale, *six* inhale, *five* exhale, *four* inhale, *three* exhale, *two* inhale, *one* exhale."

I repeated the exercise a few times, counting alternatively from one to ten and then from ten to one.

Sarah was breathing and counting mentally with me.

"Now open your eyes." I asked her how she felt.

"I feel much more relaxed," Sarah replied. "As if a weight off my chest, I feel more serene." Her face had taken on an expression of surprise.

I explained to her the reasoning behind this exercise. I like for people to understand exactly what's behind the techniques that I use, because in my opinion a relationship of trust developed by sharing all pertinent information contributes greatly to the success of any technique.

"It seems crazy, right? That just by counting breaths anxiety can be reduced?" I said.

I continued: "If I had asked you to count to twenty it would not have worked," I added, "because while our brain can count and think at the same time without problems, it can't think of other things while counting backwards! So in this way we momentarily eliminate the thoughts that cause the heightened state of anxiety. That's it. It sounds incredible, but that's how it is."

"All you need is a bit of patience," I added. "Make sure to begin again whenever a thought interrupts your backwards-counting breaths."

I invite the reader to remember this simple technique and experiment with it whenever they find themselves facing an upcoming moment of anxiety. Its effectiveness is proven and the results can be really surprising.

Sarah seemed much more relaxed now. We were ready to begin the regression. I invited her to lie down on the couch and I began inducing the trance state.

"I am wearing sandals," Sarah began. "I have dark skin. I am a woman, and I have dark and curly hair that reaches my shoulders. My dress is dirty, light in color, a tunic with a brown belt. I'm wearing a square metal buckle with silvered rivets all around me."

"Is there any detail that captures your attention?" I asked her.

"I have a corded bracelet on with many small stones attached," Sarah responded.

"How old are you?" I continued.

"Twenty-seven."

"Are you currently inside or outside?" I asked her.

"Outside, in a field. There are weeds."

"Without thinking, I want you to please tell me what year it is."

"1880," she responded, immediately.

"Where are you?"

"I'm in South Africa."

"Are there other people around you?"

"No, just Erik."

"Who is Erik?"

"My lover. We love each other but we aren't allowed to stay together because of the color of our skin. He holds me tight and sweetly strokes my face. I feel loved and protected there in his strong arms. I want to stay there forever."

"Can you describe him to me?"

"Yes. He is handsome and well dressed. He is wearing khaki pants and a white shirt. His skin is white. He has dark hair and light skin. He has to return to Europe because here he would be killed, and he wants me to go away with him. But I can't go with him, I don't want to leave my land and my people. There is a terrible war going on and I have to stay to help my loved ones. I can't abandon them. I am very sad, but I have to learn to accept things. I know he loves me and that's what counts. Our love will continue forever, even if distance separates us. Love has no set time nor expiration date. I know that we are soul mates, and I feel I've known him forever. I know that I will see him again many times in other lives. We will never really leave each other."

I saw that Sarah was crying. She was visibly upset, so I decided to bring her forward in time, to a later moment in that life.

"It's the moment of my death," Sarah said.

"A man in uniform shot me. He has a green jacket and a strange hat of the same color. He is wearing dark boots. I can clearly see his face. He has very pale skin. I also see his rifle, it has a wooden butt. He is pointing it at me now." Sarah's face had a fearful expression.

"How old are you?" I asked her.

"I'm twenty eight, it's only been one year. Erik left a few months ago."

"What's happening?"

"The soldier is shooting me. I see everything in slow motion. It hits my chest and I fall down. I can't breathe anymore."

Seeing that, even there in my office during the session, Sarah had become red in the face and she was having trouble breathing, I gave her a few hypnotic instructions to get rid of that sensation. "I'm dead now," she said. "I can breathe perfectly and see the scene from up high. My lifeless body is on the ground. I feel a sense of peace, of well-being. I feel free, although I am sad because I had to leave my people so soon without being able to help them. There are many soldiers down there, killing many people. The war is truly useless. We are all equal, all the same. When will we understand that by killing other people we are killing ourselves?"

Sarah began crying, but it was a freeing cry. She deeply understood the uselessness of war, a concept that she already knew well. After the session I discovered that she was killed during the First Boer War in the spring of 1881.

Despite the fact that Sarah didn't even know about that war, which lasted less than a year, the dates and descriptions of her story were absolutely accurate. She was even correct about the British soldiers' green jackets, a color that was worn only by the riflemen. To date, even historians have trouble providing much detail on that brief conflict.

After the sessions, I frequently do historical research and my findings confirm the strange or unusual dates or facts experienced during past life regressions. These findings would test the expertise of the most knowledgeable historians. The historical knowledge that seems so clear and simple to the person experiencing the regression is always completely unfamiliar to them just a few moments before. In my practice I have witnessed many situations in which people, often with a low level of education, report with extreme accuracy historical facts that happened hundreds of years ago in faraway places and in poorly-documented historical periods. Just as Sarah had done on that occasion. Even when I'm skeptical, as I so often was up until a few years ago, it's absolutely impossible that Sarah could have known details like the exact year, let alone the existence of that conflict, when in our day there is little coverage of the event and it isn't even studied in Sarah's country of origin, Spain.

Other than the historical correspondences, what strikes me the most about Sarah's experience is what she wrote me a few months after our meeting. She told me that anxiety didn't bother her anymore and that remembering that past life had allowed her to understand the importance of caring for her loved ones in her present life. And, even though it was the middle of August, she told me that only a few minutes after the session the asthma that had plagued her for years had completely disappeared.

Even after years of practice, I'm still surprised by the power that regression can have in resolving our problems. It's as if our brain really has the power to tap into memories that come from elsewhere, in another space or time, but that also condition its behavior. This would be confirmed by the "Orchestrated Objective Reduction (Orch-OR)" theory of quantum physics on microtubules and consciousness, which the American doctor Dr. Stuart Hameroff, director of the Center for Consciousness Studies in Arizona and Roger Penrose, mathematical physicist and emeritus professor of the University of Oxford have been working on since 1996. According to this theory, there is no real separation between that what is inside us and outside of us. Consciousness finds itself in both places. Our brain, like a complex computer that uses a wireless network, seems to be able to receive documents and programs coming from outside that permit it to function in a more efficient way. As if at the precise moment of our death we were simply exchanging an old computer for a new one, the old machine turns off but the information and the consciousness remain in the universe, ready to be used in the new computer, in our new life.

Having relived the experience of her own death in that past life, Sarah was able to free herself from the memory that didn't have anything to do with her actual existence. She was able to understand in an immediate and direct way that the heavy feeling in her chest and the difficulty breathing that had characterized her life up until that moment came from being shot in a past life. Sarah was finally able to feel the joy of taking in a full breath of air.

"You use hypnosis not as a cure but as a means of establishing a favorable climate in which to learn."
Milton H. Erickson

CONSCIOUSNESS AND THE BRAIN

On a pleasant summer afternoon, I was standing on the terrace of a young director's apartment in Rome, celebrating his fortieth birthday party on the invitation of a mutual friend. The terrace, which was full of decorative fruit-bearing plants, looked out onto an immense garden with ancient and thriving trees amongst the green of that elegant residential Roman neighborhood. The owner seemed to have a talent for decoration, and just like the rest of the house, the terrace was tastefully done. Among the various pieces of furniture were two marvelous ceramic armchairs from the 1900s with roaring lion heads on the arm rests. They were perfectly conserved. I thought they must have cost a fortune, but I was wrong. The owner of the house explained to me that they were a gift given to his parents by the old owner, whom they had met in the licentious 1960s when they lived together in a small *art nouveau* villa just down the street from where we were.

Once again I had made a snap judgement, the fruit of my preconceptions. I still had much to learn, I reminded myself. It's my Ego's fault. It's always been ready to jump to hasty conclusions.

And it was the Ego that we ended up talking about that night. It was the umpteenth proof that chance didn't exist and that the Universe, or God, or Allah, or Nature, the Cosmos, Energy—whatever you want to call it—was taking advantage of my life events to teach me something new. I found myself seated in front of the splendid panorama of Roman roofs, with an excellent gin and tonic aromatized with ginger to sip on, happy to be out of the way. I had felt a little out of place since the beginning of the party, because I wasn't accustomed to elite events; furthermore, living abroad and dealing with a controversial subject like past lives, I had immediately become the center of attention of the other guests, friends of the owner of the house, actors in Roman theatre and cinema, professionals, and people of culture. I felt observed, a sensation that had awakened in me a slight social anxiety. In that moment I looked at how the sun, at this point low on the horizon, created flashes of pink light among the thriving plants. I thought that, if I lived there, that terrace would be an ideal place to practice my daily meditation. I was enjoying a moment of peace and reflection, placidly seated. The girl seated next to me in the ceramic chair was seemingly doing the same.

"So you really deal with past lives?" Julia asked me suddenly, breaking the silence. A pseudonym of her own choosing, Julia is a young and relatively well-known director of Roman theatre. She later told me that she chose this pseudonym in honor of the female protagonist of "1984," the famous book by George Orwell, but in that moment I thought it was because of her exceptional resemblance to Julia Roberts. She had the same haircut and hair color, shoulder-length and reddish brunette. Her sweet features and eyes were also within striking distance of that famous *Oscar* and *Golden Globe* winner. She only wore a bit of makeup: black eyeliner and pink lip gloss that rendered justice to her perfectly formed lips. She was dressed in a serious and elegant manner. She wore a black dress that wrapped her body and arrived just above her knee and a short jacket, red, that nicely defined her waist. I was struck by the large brooch pinned on her jacket, an unusual detail for a woman of her age. It was a mosaic shaped like a peacock, made up of many stones of various colors. It was a bit of character that wouldn't have bewildered the same Julia Roberts, and that revealed the slightly eccentric nature of this Roman Julia, a characteristic leftover from her past as an actress.

Julia didn't know it, but that day she was still simply a marionette of her own ego, as we all are until we become aware of it. She still had many things to discover, about herself, about human nature, and about how she went beyond a mere material existence. To use a metaphor, often quoted by the same Dr. Weiss and more than appropriate for the context of that night, I think that all of us are theatrical characters and that our earthly life represents a scene, at the end of which the actors leave their character and return home.

"Yes," I responded, "I've dedicated myself to past life regression therapy for years."

"Come on!" Julia said, trying to hide an amused snicker. "Pardon my frankness, but I really don't believe in these things. I'm an atheist and don't believe in reincarnation."

"I used to think the same as you," I responded, "but I had to change my mind. I assisted in the experiences of many people who have recounted really incredible things."

"Of course, people are afraid to die and they need to believe in something," said Julia.

"Have you ever meditated?" I asked her, "Have you read any Buddhist texts?"

"Don't talk to me about religions, they really aren't for me," she responded. "But I think I've had experiences similar to meditation. You know, in theatre class we do visualization exercises that seem pretty similar to meditation techniques, as far as I know."

"So you accept that there can be more than one mental state?" I asked.

"Well, yes. I think so. But it's my brain that decides what to visualize. Even when I do the exercises in theater, it sometimes seems like my thoughts shut off and everything appears clearer."

"I don't think it's only a fear of death," I said. "It is a human necessity to explain ourselves, to seek out our origins. The eternal question to which man has not yet found the response: Who are we and where do we come from?"

"If man explains himself, it's as if he were observing himself from the outside. Is that why you asked me if I was able to meditate? Why, when we do the visualization exercises in theatre, do I get the sensation that one part of me observes the other?" asked Julia, curiously.

"Yes, exactly like that. You just described self-awareness. An eternal debate. It was discussed in Freud's era, with his *Id/Ego/Superego*, but the subject has been taken on by many philosophers since antiquity. It's a complicated question that even in our day deals with psychology, philosophy, religion, and many other disciplines. And the element around which the entire question revolves, in my opinion, is precisely the concept of self-awareness, a characteristic that neuroscientists only recognize in man and a small number of other animal species," I responded.

"If it's how you say, it seems like it's primarily a scientific argument that has to do with psychology and the functionality of human beings. I don't see anything transcendental about it," replied Julia, reminding me that I found myself in front of a truly convinced materialist.

"Let's not forget that the meaning of the word *psyche* in ancient Greek is soul. So psychology is really the study of the soul. It was only later that the meaning was changed to 'mind.' As you can see, this has been an open question for quite some time. I'm not ashamed to give my opinion, seeing as how the workings of the brain, above all regarding the conscious, are a great mystery even today, even for neuroscientists. We were able to attribute concrete functions to the various regions of the brain but we still can't explain exactly how it works. It really is gray matter!" I laughed to myself about the joke, while Julia continued to look at me with a serious and attentive expression.

"There is a scientific theory that explains how our conscious experiences are the result of quantum gravity inside microtubules, tiny structures of the neurons' cytoskeleton." I tried to explain the Penrose and Hameroff theory, which I briefly described at the end of the last chapter, according to which consciousness is both material and non-material, metaphorically the computer and the software, and that even science itself was beginning to hypothesize that consciousness could exist outside of the brain.

"How cool," exclaimed Julia, "it's like *The Matrix*," alluding to the famous movie from 1990.

Now that I was able to capture her interest, the girl looked at me with respect. I had used a scientific basis to support my reasoning. Maybe, in her eyes, I stopped seeming like a slightly crazy middle-aged man.

"It's exactly like *The Matrix*," I replied. "The reality that we perceive on a daily basis is just an illusion, an interpretation that our brain attributes to sensorial stimuli. In changing these stimuli one can literally change reality. So, the conscience would seem to be the product of external stimuli—the software—interpreted by the brain—the computer. A recent experiment explains simply what I'm talking about. A visual software visor (a piece of technology that today is available to everyone, thanks to the *immersive* technology of Google Cardboard) was put on a person lying down on a couch. Connected to the visor was a video camera on top of a Barbie doll's head. The person saw the Barbie doll's body where their own should be, and if they raised or lowered their gaze, they saw the legs or bust of the Barbie doll. When the scientist in charge of the experiment touched the participant's leg, he simultaneously touched the corresponding Barbie leg. In that moment the subject began to identify with the doll, recognizing the Barbie leg as part of their own body. The illusion was so real that the person began perceiving the objects around them as much larger and farther away than they were.

The scientist's finger or pencil that touched their leg was now perceived as enormous and heavy."

"Incredible," commented Julia.

"Yes, really incredible," I responded. "And that's what we do in the first few months of our lives. We identify with our bodies and our brains, just like the person in the experiment did with the doll. While in reality we are much more than a body and a brain. If you really don't want to call it a *soul*, can I at least call it *information?*" I asked her, chuckling.

"Fine," the girl said, smiling at me.

The conversation had become pleasant. One could tell that the young woman was a curious person, with a critical spirit and an open mind.

"Think of a newborn baby in his first few months of life," I said. "Initially he cries and laughs while he looks at his mom, his dad, the house, and the world around him. But he is still not conscious of the fact that he is a separate entity from the rest. For him, mom, dad, his crib, and the world around him are the same thing, an immense sea without separation. He is still not conscious of himself, he doesn't have self-awareness. And that's exactly how it is. The information, or soul, has only recently entered his brain and is beginning to be developed. The child, up until about six months old, has not yet constructed or circumscribed the limits of his own body. He still doesn't know what it is, just like the experiment with the doll. And he isn't wrong. Because, as we have seen, the limits of the body are a mere illusion. Physics explain how in reality the atoms that compose everything, including the human body, are composed of even smaller particles, the smallest and most elementary, called fermions, that are communal to every type of material. The differences between things, whether they are objects or animals, are attributed to different combinations of the same identical particles. Even air is composed of the same micro-particles that our body is made up of. That means that there is no separation between the baby's body and the mom's, and the same thing applies to dad, the crib, and the rest of the world. The newborn is not wrong, we are wrong. Even at a material level we are all the same thing. Between my brain, my skull, the air that separates us, your brain, and your skull, there is no real separation on a material level. We should stop considering ourselves to be different entities and, rather than focus on the differences, embrace our similarities. We are all the same thing. We should finally realize this and stop judging or hating our neighbor because we consider him different from us. Numerous psychometric experiments have attempted to show that we could even possess telepathic capabilities because the information that we draw from is the same. And if we add to that the nanoparticles of quantum mechanics, then from a non-material point of view, we are all made up of the same information. I use this term to make you happy, Julia, but otherwise I'd gladly use the word 'soul.'"

"This is crazy! You're giving me a headache. I don't know who I am anymore. Can we get another drink?" said Julia jokingly.

I accepted the invitation but limited myself to a tonic water. I don't like to abuse alcohol, because I had the opportunity to study in-depth the devastating effects it can provoke on the precious neurons that we're discussing.

We went inside the house, because it was dark by now and it was getting colder on the terrace. We went to sit on a large white leather couch, where some poor people had to listen to our conversation, demonstrating interest in the argument that we were debating.

"So then why do we feel like flesh and bone?" Julia asked me.

It seemed that, without even realizing it, she was already taking for granted that we were more than just a body.

"It's all our Ego's fault," I responded. And I added, "I am referring to the definition that Buddhists give for Ego. Otherwise we risk confusing it with the term *Ego*, which Freud used to describe another part of the mind. I don't know how much you know about psychology, but the Buddhist Ego might correspond more to the Freudian *Superego*, or to the *Observer* of the post-rationalists, and thus to the concept of self-consciousness explored in our day by modern neuroscientists."

I explained to her that I had dedicated much of my free time to the study of psychology and that, even though I possessed a postgraduate diploma in Clinical Psychopathology with a cognitive-behavioral focus, I had always remained faithful to my initial Jungian psychoanalytical experience. In fact, according to Jung, the *Ego* is the conscious part of the personality, the subject of all conscious actions.

The Ego is a completely separate part of the subconscious that, even if it's totally ignored by cognitive behavioral therapists, in reality makes up an integral part of our being.

The Ego is a true illusion. It's a product of the brain that, in order to legitimize its own existence, needs to proclaim its independence from the rest of the world. When a child who is a few months old first sees the fingers on his little hand move, he understands that he controls its movement and thus begins the identification of the Ego. The deed is done. The spiritual and infinite being that we are becomes closed in a shell of flesh and bone, prisoner of its own Ego. It's a tyrant that doesn't leave room for our true, peaceful nature.

Often, when I see a newborn cry, I think they have every reason in the world to do so and I wonder if that cry doesn't express the desperation of a being that, having just left his divine nature behind, finds himself immobile and constrained in a limited terrestrial body. And also, if I may, at the mercy of dirty diapers, belly aches, and an inability to communicate.

"With the passage of time, our Ego gains more and more control, to the detriment of our true being, that creature of peace that we really are, with whom we are able to connect during regressions or meditation. That's why I asked you in the beginning if you had ever tried to meditate."

"Actually, when I do visualization exercises I feel much more serene. I feel an almost surreal sense of peace," said Julia.

"It's because with those exercises, which are quite similar to a meditation, you are able to perceive what you really are, without the thousands of thoughts that your brain and your Ego produces to keep you busy," I explained to her. "You are not your brain," I added.

"Wow! I feel like I never stop thinking. If only I could,"

the girl replied.

"Think of how our brain, dominated by the Ego, produces sixty thousands thoughts every day!" I said. Then I asked her, "In your case, are the majority of these thoughts intentional or do they come on their own?"

"They come on their own," she said, "I don't decide to think those things."

"So, if you don't produce them intentionally, what produces them?" I said, "So then you and your brain are not the same entity. Or, better yet, there are two entities coexisting in your brain. The conscious and the self-conscious. The *Ego* and *Superego*. The *Observer* and the *Observed*. The Ego and the Being. Call them what you want. And are the majority of these sixty thousand thoughts negative or positive?" I continued.

"Umm..." Julia reflected, "I would say negative."

"You're not alone," I told her, "It's the same for all of us. The majority of thoughts that our Ego produces are negative ones. It's a way of exercising control. It constantly moves us towards future worries, which are the root of our anxiety, and past regrets, which generate sensations of guilt and prevent us from acting. And moving constantly between the future and the past robs us of the ability to decide in the only moment in which we really can do so. The only moment in which we are free: the Now.

It's a tyrant who makes its own decisions and tells us in every moment what we should do, if we acted well, and how we should have acted. That doesn't leave space for our true Being, an entity of peace and infinite love, devoid of worries, judgements, preconceived notions, and suffering."

"You're describing me as a schizophrenic," Julia said, now sounding worried. "How can I free myself from this monster in my head?"

"Don't worry," I chuckled, "Schizophrenia is something totally different. This 'monster,' as you call it, is something we all have and unfortunately it moves us like puppets in whichever direction it wants. But I have good news. Now that you've realized your own existence, you are already at a good point. You can begin your great interior revolution. You can finally understand that, because you are not your brain, you can react totally autonomously from it. You don't necessarily have to agree with the thoughts that it produces, with the directives that it gives you, or with what it decides is right or wrong. Knowing how to recognize them, you can decide to evaluate or abandon any one of these thoughts. Welcome to your new life, free from tyranny!"

"Craziness," Julia said. "I had never thought of it. I always thought I was the origin of my thoughts and up until now I always assumed responsibility and fault."

"I've said all this to explain to you what happens during a past-life regression," I told her. "Simply, using a hypnotic induction, an altered state of consciousness can be reached, during which we seek to establish a perfect equilibrium in which these two parts can coexist, reaching a state in which the Ego is not the master."

"You know what I think?" Julia said. "I want to try. Will you still be in Rome tomorrow evening? Do you want to come to my house and try? My husband is a chef and he is off tomorrow. What do you think?"

My Ego decided to accept, motivated perhaps by the hunger re-awakened now that it was dinner time, or perhaps by the challenge that Julia presented: converting a convinced materialist and atheist.

"Okay," I said. And we both moved towards the giant table, luxuriously set, where we separated because the Universe, or perhaps simply the party organizers, decreed that that evening we would sit at different sides of the large table.

The following evening, despite Julia's materialist, atheist and completely earthly attitude, the regression experience proved to be one of the most complete and accurate that I've ever assisted in.

I arrived at Julia's house in a rental car and I remember that, in order to get to her house, I drove a long time through her Roman neighborhood near the Tiber river. It was a popular neighborhood at the time, especially among the young and intellectual types in Rome. Julia's house fit perfectly into the tastes of that demographic. It was furnished in an industrial shabby-chic style, uniting industrial structures in cold tones with vintage, refurbished furniture. I should have expected as much, after all she was an artist and she had travelled a lot, so of course the furnishings in her house would be avant-garde. She opened the door and greeted me with a huge smile. Behind her there was a huge library full of books new and old, which I thought unusual for someone of her age. If that house struck me so much, it was probably because my tiny studio near the sea was forcibly feng shui, with no room to accumulating books. I had to limit myself to the essentials. My hundreds of books are now housed in a small *Kindle* e-reader that I bring with me wherever I go. I didn't have the courage to admit that to Julia, who, like a good intellectual, I think would have lost all respect for me.

"Make yourself comfortable," she told me. "Let me introduce you to Sebastian, my husband."

"Nice to meet you," I responded. "Julia told me a lot about you and your cooking. Thank you for inviting me."

Sebastian was the same age as his wife. He was tall and thin, with brown hair that was going a little grey despite his youth. A simple dark shirt and jeans completed his look. His calm personality greatly compensated for Julia's energetic one.

"We've prepared a totally vegetarian menu for you," Sebastian said, jokingly. "Julia told me about the acrobatics you did with your silverware last night to separate the vegetables from the food you really wanted to eat," said Sebastian, in a joking way.

He was a nice guy. His vaguely British sense of humor won me over.

Besides, his vegan spring rolls were brilliant and testified not only to his abilities as a chef, but to the fact that one can eat an exquisite meal even without animal products.

We finished dinner early and the time after dinner was dedicated to the regression. Sebastian retreated to his studio and left us in the living room. I asked Julia if we could explore some episode of her childhood before going on to a past life, and she consented. It's a method that I often use with more rational people, in which the left hemisphere of the brain doesn't readily permit us to leave the material and terrestrial world. Going to a childhood episode is a little "trick" that lets the brain think it's in complete control. After all, it deals with earthly and thus controllable memories, even if the evidence shows that many childhood memories that emerge during regressions correspond to real but forgotten episodes. I asked Julia to lie down comfortably on the couch and I asked her to put on the EEG headset. The headset is an instrument that, when connected to my laptop, measures the cerebral activity of the subject. That's how I was able to monitor, at every moment, the profundity of the hypnotic state that she reached that evening.

So we began with the induction. Halfway through I realized that Julia had already reached a deep trance state. Her eyes, which had begun to move rapidly behind her closed eyelids, teared up without her realizing and her body became completely rigid.

"Where are you?" I asked her.

"I'm at my parents' house."

"How old are you?"

"I'm about four. I am sitting at a table with my grandmother. She is smiling at me. Our dog is also there, a female Yorkshire Terrier mix. She seems so large to me now, even though in reality she was small. It's me who is small. Even grandma is big. I can perfectly see all the details of my house. The couch has an ugly blue floral print to it. It's early afternoon and my grandmother is with me because my parents are still at work, but they're about to come home. I feel very happy with her."

"Are there any other details that capture your attention?"

"Yes. Grandma's dress. I can see it perfectly. I hadn't remembered it. It's light brown with tiny geometric designs, little black squares."

"What is happening now?" I asked her, seeing that the

girl's expression had changed.

"My parents came home. Grandma left and I don't feel calm anymore."

"Why aren't you calm?"

"I'm afraid to do something wrong. Whatever I do, I'm afraid to appear fragile in front of them. I'm afraid to fail. I can't do anything for fear of doing something wrong."

"Are they very hard to please?" I asked her

"No, quite the opposite," responded Julia. "Everything I do is fine with them. They always tell me that I'm good, no matter what I do. It's precisely for that reason that I feel fragile and afraid. If everything is always fine, how will I know what is wrong and what is right? I prefer not to do anything."

"I understand," I reassured her, knowing that her insecurity didn't come from her parents but was rooted in something much farther away. Reliving this episode would have freed her from the fear of doing wrong. That's the great power that a single regression can have.

"Now, if you agree, I'd like to go back even further in time," and I began to guide her to a past life.

"It's nice. It's dark. It's cold," began Julia, who started to tremble.

"Where are you?" I asked her.

"It seems like the deck of some big harbor. There is an enormous building in front of me. I'm at the corner of the pier and I can easily read the writing on the building. It says 'Todd Pacific Corporation,' I think."

"How are you dressed?"

"I'm wearing black men's shoes and light wool pants, well made. I must be rich. My shirt is clean and ironed and I have a jacket which is also high quality."

"How is your hair?"

"Short, brown and combed back but…I'm a woman! I'm wearing men's clothes but I am a woman! Even my hands are women's hands. Damn!"

"What is your name?"

"My name is Janet. Janet Browning," she said.

"How old are you?"

"About forty," Julia answered, without hesitation.

"Where are you? What year is it?"

"I'm at the San Francisco Harbor. It's 1942, I think."

"What are you doing there?"

"I am waiting for someone."

"Who are you waiting for?"

"I'm waiting for my lover."

"Who is he?"

"No, no. She. I think I'm a lesbian," the girl said, chuckling at her own surprise. "Her name is Sarah," she added. "Sarah Todd."

"Todd is the name on the building, correct?"

"Yes, it's her family's building. They own ships. But they had to convert the shipyard into a supply depot for the war. There's a war on. The Second World War. Sarah's father is against our love and he has forbidden her to see me. He made her marry a man but she continues to see me in secret."

"How do you feel? What are you feeling?"

"I am happy because soon I will see her but sad at the same time. I remember that a few years ago, before Sarah got married, I went to go speak with her father and tried to explain the situation to him. He insulted me ferociously and treated me very badly. He had his workers throw me out and they treated me without respect, almost like an animal. I am a strong and self-assured woman."

"You are very much in love with Sarah?"

"Yes, I love her a lot. Always. But I've also been angry with her. I scolded her because she didn't have the courage to react. She totally gave in to what her family wanted, what her father and brother wanted. I feel a lot of resentment towards them."

"How is Sarah? Can you describe her for me?"

"She is very beautiful. At least to me. She's young, eight years younger than I am, with delicate features and marvelous blue eyes. She moves sweetly and smiles at me. She is very feminine, a true lady. She is wearing a light tailleur style dress with a leather belt that wraps tightly around her waist and shows off her marvelous hips. She also has a little cap or maybe a bow that gathers her long blonde hair. She's so elegant. I feel proud to be the object of her love."

"Look deeply into her eyes and tell me if you feel that in Sarah's body there could be the soul of a person that Julia knows in her current life," I asked her, as I always do in these cases.

"Oh, God, yes! It's Sebastian! My love!" Julia said, crying tears of joy.

Once again I found myself in front of two soul mates. These two beings have loved each other forever and have shared numerous existences, playing multiple varied roles, as they continued to do as Janet and Sarah.

"How did you meet Sarah?" I asked her.

"I met her when we were young. When I arrived in America from Scotland, where I was born in a small village called Ayrshire, I had a fling with Sarah's brother. Then I fell in love with Sarah."

"Are you married?"

"Yes."

"What is your husband like?"

"He's an elegant man, also probably very rich. Seeing his clothes and thinking what our house is like, I can say without a doubt he must be rich. He is beside me right now."

"Can you look him in the eyes, please?" I asked her.

"It's my brother. I feel certain that the soul of my husband in Janet's life is the same one as my brother in my current life. Julia's brother. It's incredible!"

"Where are you both?"

"A few years have passed and we are entering our house. It's the evening. I get the inescapable feeling that it's the moment of my death."

"And how do you die? How old are you?"

"Only a few years have passed, so I'm still young. While we are walking home to our elegant house in San Francisco, a man with a pistol comes over to us. It's Sarah's brother. He points the gun at me and he looks into my eyes under the astonished gaze of my husband, who is unable to do anything. As he shoots me I see in Sarah's brother's eyes that he respects me, that he respects my choice. I know that he would never have wanted to do it, even if he resents me because I broke up with him years ago because of my relationship with Sarah. His family forced him to do this. He is shooting me."

Julia's face became tense and her legs began to move by themselves.

"I feel my legs trembling. I can't believe that I am

really going to die right now. I didn't expect it." She began to cry. "I'm sorry I was not able to do the things I wanted to do, when I was Janet."

"What is it like to die?" I asked her then.

"It's wonderful. I've left Janet's body, now. I feel light and I'm not suffering anymore. Actually I'm very serene. I've just died but I feel tranquil. I feel at peace." Her legs stopped moving and her face relaxed.

"You can leave Janet's life now." I prompted her, "What have you learned from that life?"

"I've learned that I'm strong and that now I possess all the characteristics and capacities to make decisions. As Julia, I now have the opportunity to do what I want. Janet was denied that opportunity. I have to take advantage of it. I have to react."

"What's happening now?"

"I'm going up. I see the streets and the city from up high. My husband is stroking my face. Sarah's brother isn't running away. He seems almost upset, astonished by what he just did. I keep going up and up. I feel so light and happy. I go up near the clouds. A word keeps bouncing around in my head—*Courage!*—and I keep going up. Now I'm among the clouds and I hear that someone is coming. It's a male presence. I'm not scared, and actually it's strangely familiar to me, even if neither Julia nor Janet knew him directly. But I feel as if I've known him forever. I feel that he loves me. I know that his name is David and perhaps he is my guide, a type of guardian angel." And she laughed at what she, a convinced materialist, had just said.

"Does he have some message for you?" I asked.

"Yes. He doesn't speak. It's as if he is repeating the

same message with every fiber of his being: *It's time!*"

As soon as the girl finished saying those words, something truly incredible happened and I felt adrenaline suddenly pass through my body. On my computer screen I saw the data relative to Julia's cerebral activity, measured by the EEG headset that she was wearing, show predominantly delta waves for a moment or two. Delta waves are not predominant in a waking state, but only appear during a deep sleep, general anesthesia, or some states of a coma. But in that moment Julia was right in front of me and she certainly wasn't sleeping!

I was in a state of shock. Those waves should never present in a situation like that one. It was as if her brain was effectively processing data autonomously from the conscious mind, as if in that moment she was receiving soul-like information from an external source. It seemed that it wasn't Julia talking, but her soul.

"That *information* you were talking about earlier, the *soul* as you call it..." the girl started to say, "It's made up of love. Just love. It's the only energy that exists. Nothing else. Love is everything."

This last affirmation didn't surprise me at all. I have conducted hundreds of regressions and nearly everyone mentioned love as the only existing form of energy, that joins us together with everyone else and everything there is. Even in the eyes of someone like me who doesn't embrace any terrestrial religion, the love described by those experiencing a regression is very similar to the concept of God.

I observed the girl's body and noted that she had relaxed and her face had taken on an expression of total bliss. I decided it was time to wake her up and bring her back to the couch in her house; that evening I had permitted her to travel through space and time.

The following year I had the opportunity to speak with Julia to see if her regression had any effect on her life. We did so in a hypnosis session in which she asked me to help her stop smoking, being now convinced of the power of the hypnotic technique. She told me that the theatre production she had directed that year in Rome had been very successful. And, thanks to her courage and renewed capacities, the acting school she directed had undertaken new, great initiatives. She didn't blush anymore and she didn't diminish herself and pretend it was no big deal when someone gave her a compliment. In fact now she accepted compliments joyfully, convinced that she deserved them. Even her love story with Sebastian was strengthened and stabilized, because now Julia knew that he was her true soul mate, the one who had always been and would always be beside her. Now she was a daring woman!

She told me that she discovered on the internet that Todd Naval Industries really did exist in that period and that they were converted into wartime supply producers. She also told me she found the birth record of Janet Browning, born in the village of Ayrshire in Scotland in 1901, and that of Sarah Todd, born in 1909 in the United States. She found tangible proof her rational and completely earthly mind so desired.

Julia's experience reminds us of the infinite capacities of our mind, or maybe the soul itself, that can bring us back to the crucial moments that markedly altered our existence. As in Julia's childhood, when she was afraid to mess up and thought she couldn't do anything. She still carried these sensations with her from Janet's existence, when she did not have the ability to choose or do what she wanted. The destiny denied to Janet would have still frustrated Julia, were it not for the regression that allowed her to understand how those limits, those invisible chains, were caused by events that had nothing to do with her present life. Her current existence was now full of great successes.

"Even the enlightened person is never more than his own limited ego before the One who dwells within him, whose form has no knowable boundaries, who encompasses him on all sides, fathomless as the abysms of the earth and vast as the sky."
Carl Gustav Jung

PARENTS AND CHILDREN

My heart sank when I got the call from Aurora. I was at home, making something for dinner, and the phone rang. After a certain hour I always turn off my computer and cellphone and I don't answer calls or read emails. I prefer to spend my evenings surrounded by calm, helping me to re-energize for the next day. I don't even listen to music, as it would interrupt the absolute silence.

Just to confirm that there truly is no such thing as a coincidence, that night I had forgotten to turn off my phone.

"Hello?" I answered.

"Hello?" replied a female voice quivering through tears. "Can I talk to Alex?"

"That's me."

"My name is Aurora. I'm sorry to bother you at this hour, but I would like to make an appointment with you. It's very urgent."

"Don't worry," I said, touched by the woman's tears. I get many calls from people who believe they have an urgent problem, although usually the extent of the urgency involved has been something of a subjective matter. So, to ensure I keep an egalitarian and professional approach towards everyone who calls me, before I make an appointment I ask for clarification on the nature of their problem, in order to decide if there's a specific need to help this person before the others.

"What happened?" I therefore asked.

"My baby died, my little Nicholas!" said the sobbing woman. "He had just turned two months old. He was fine and suddenly he passed away. I can't live anymore. Please help me!" she said. Then she burst into never-ending tears.

"Could you come by tomorrow?" I suggested when the tears subsided.

There was no time to lose, that woman really needed help. There is no greater pain than the loss of a child, be it in the womb, a baby, an adolescent or adult. It's not part of the order of earthly things, those we can understand and control, though sometimes this kind of tragedy can be part of a design that's bigger than us. I'm not a father myself, but in past lives I have lost children and, though the pain is not as excruciating in this existence, the memory of those events continues to exist, like an echo in my soul.

"At what time?" the woman asked.

"One o'clock," I answered, identifying the only free moment of the day. I would have to skip lunch, but the gravity of these events left me no choice.

"Thank you so much, I truly don't know how to thank you," Aurora said, with a now slightly calmed tone of voice.

After the encounter, a strange feeling pervaded my mind and body. Although I had just spoken with a distraught woman and heard all her profound sadness, I felt serene. Life had given me the opportunity to do good.

It was a feeling I was familiar with but which I recently discovered has a scientific basis. A recent study by the School of Medicine at Stanford University showed that compassion towards others produces enormous benefits, contributing to our psychological and physiological well-being.

That phone call, which according to my plan for the evening was disturbing my peace, had instead given me a greater serenity.

The next day, when I opened the door, I was confronted with a completely different woman from the sad and scared little creature I expected to meet after talking to her on the phone the night before. Aurora was a tall and shapely woman. She had long, black hair, curly and rebellious. She had pronounced cheekbones and her fully, rosy cheeks might have suggested a Viking origin were it not for her Mediterranean complexion. She was well dressed and made up perfectly. I intuited that she was trying to make a good impression and use makeup to mask the pain that her tired, lifeless eyes communicated at that difficult time in her life.

"Thank you for seeing me," she said, with a sudden embrace I couldn't avoid.

I never encourage physical contact and it always makes me feel a little embarrassed. It's not out of coldness or a lack of empathy, but more a relic I carry from my psychoanalytic experience, because any type of contact between therapist and patient is absolutely not recommended.

"Thank you, Aurora, for your trust. Have a seat," I said with a reassuring smile.

I invited her to sit at the desk to tell me about her experience.

"It happened two weeks ago. We were at home. Me, my husband, and my oldest son, aged nine. My husband and I were in the kitchen and Nicholas' crib was next to us. I was preparing dinner while my husband watched TV. Nicholas seemed to be sleeping peacefully. But I realized something strong was going on. I kept turning around to look at him while I was preparing dinner, and it seemed like for a few minutes Nicholas had stayed in the exact some position. A strange feeling alerted me and made me leave dinner to rush to his crib. There I discovered that Nicholas wasn't breathing anymore. I screamed in panic and my husband called the ambulance. I remained motionless for a few moments while my husband called and waited for help, then I tried to revive him in every possible way, but it didn't help. Within a few minutes my beautiful baby had left us," Aurora said through tears and sobs.

"I am so sorry," I said as soon as she had finished crying. I asked if the doctors were able to establish a cause of death for little Nicholas.

"They only said that his little heart stopped. Nothing more. They thought it might be SIDS, Sudden Infant Death Syndrome. There was no apparent cause, which makes my despair that much worse. I don't understand why it happened. And why it had to happen to me. I can't have any peace. I'm taking sedatives but I still can't sleep at night," she explained with what was now a flat voice. "Please help me," she then added.

"I hope I can. I truly hope I can," I replied. And I was terribly sincere.

I proceeded to explain the methodology I used, then asked her the usual questions to prepare for the session, and invited her to lie on the couch and we proceeded immediately to the regression.

"I see my shoes, women's shoes, short ankle boots. I'm wearing a long dress, decorated with lace, gray, narrow at the waist. My collar is in the Asian style, closed by buttons. I have light brown hair, gathered behind my neck. I think I'm rich, dressed as a woman of class."

"Where are you," I asked.

"I'm at my house. Sitting in an armchair. I'm embroidering and next to me is a young man reading the newspaper, sitting at a large and luxurious wooden desk. He is my son. I must be about forty-five years old and he seems to be around twenty. I feel I love him very much, and I have dedicated my life to him. He grew up with all the love and attention he could possibly have. Now he is a talented young man, studying at the university."

"Can you look at him carefully and describe him, please?" I asked the woman.

"He is dressed elegantly, with a white shirt and bowtie. The elegant clothes highlight his blond hair and blue eyes." The woman paused before exclaiming "Oh God! It's my little Nicholas! I recognize Nicholas, it's the same soul in two different lives!"

Aurora burst into tears again and cried without end, but this time it was tears of joy and emotion. I let her enjoy her baby son.

After a few minutes her expression darkened. She had stopped crying but seemed concerned.

"What happened?" I asked.

"It is late afternoon, nearly dark. I'm walking quickly down the street, on the sidewalk. I have a brown leather bag, wearing a very elaborate hat with a wide brim. I get the impression that I'm following someone."

"You're following someone or someone is following you?"

"No. It's me who is following someone. A young man. I know I know him but he does not know me."

"Where are you?"

"Chicago, the United States."

"Do you live there?"

"Yes."

"What year is it?"

"It is 1902."

"Who is the young man you are following?"

"It's my other son. But he doesn't know it. He is about 22 years old. He was born of an affair and I could not keep him because I was already married when I got pregnant. After him I had another son, the one I saw before in my house, who is smaller and could grow. My husband discovered that affair and made me give away the child, and that child is who I'm following. So I wouldn't have to have an abortion I left the city in the last months of my pregnancy, we lived in New York at that time. We are very rich. My husband is a businessman, he works in trade with Europe. I've never loved him, but I was forced to marry him; our families belong to the English upper class and ours is not a marriage between people but between business interests. He has always respected me as I respect him, but we do not love one another. He has had and still has many women."

"Why are you following your illegitimate son?"

"I've only just managed to learn where I could find him. I had to bribe officials and even a few unscrupulous nuns to find out where he was. He was adopted by a family of criminals. They have used him since childhood for their sinister activities, driving him into crime. I'm risking a lot to follow him, but I want to see him. I want to see my son."

Suddenly Aurora's body stiffened. The expression on her face became tense and worried and her skin turned red.

"What's going on?" I asked, curious.

"He just turned and walked down an alley. He is pointing a gun at another man. I am very scared. I cannot believe that my son is so cruel. He looks like a criminal. He seems to be trying to rob that man. Oh no!"

"What's going on?" I asked again, seeing her face taking on an expression of pure terror.

"The other man pulled out a gun. And he shot my son, who has now fallen to the ground. I think he's dying. I can't help but reach for him, heedless of the danger of trying to rescue him while the murderer is running away."

"Look into your son's eyes, please, and tell me if his soul belongs to someone you can recognize as Aurora, in your current life," I then asked, knowing we could be faced with another surprise.

"Yes. I know him. It's my son in my current life, in Aurora's life. The nine-year-old."

"Good," I said. "He too has come back to you, in this life."

"Yes, he has!" she replied in a surprised tone.

"I feel so happy now," she continued, "Even if he is dead I will see him again. He has come back to me. Just like Nicholas did."

Her expression brightened considerably: During that past life she had witnessed the death of her son, yet she knew that he had come back to share his current life with her. At that precise moment, in the present, he was waiting at home. Aurora had also realized that the soul of little Nicholas, who died prematurely in this life, was with her and always accompanied her.

Nicholas continues to be part of her family in heaven, the numerous souls with whom we share our multiple earthly experiences, with which we learn our lessons and learn about love, compassion, and respect towards others and all forms of life.

They would subsequently guide Aurora at the moment of her death, which occurred without any trauma. After the death of little Nicholas he manifested to her in soul form. He revealed that he continued to protect her at all times from the place where she now found him.

Nicholas has already had the opportunity to share a long and happy life with her, and he had been able to experience her maternal love in depth. Something that had been lacking in his brother, an illegitimate child in the other life. His departure, at only two months old, took the form of a grand gesture of love towards his brother. He had come back to life for a brief moment, reminding Aurora of the strength of their eternal and unbreakable bond.

That day, Aurora left feeling much more peaceful than when she had arrived just a few hours earlier. I was able to talk with her a few weeks later and she confirmed that she was recomposing her life, fully enjoying every moment spent with her other son of nine, knowing that Nicholas was always next to them.

The story of Aurora teaches us that, in our lives, even the events which seem full of sadness and suffering can actually be part of a grand design whose sole purpose is to share an eternal and unbreakable love.

However, to understand what it means to be a parent, you don't need to have children yourself, as we can see through the experience of Isabel, the woman I will speak of now. Her regression remains a unique event for me, even after the hundreds of experiences I have been able to assist with.

Isabel is a 44-year-old woman, although when I saw her I thought she must have been at least ten years younger. She looked like something out of a fashion magazine. She was tall and beautiful. Her soft features married perfectly with her Mediterranean nature and her long black hair reaching halfway down her back, smooth and glimmering. She wore glasses, but even these gave her something more, framing the beauty of her lightly almond-shaped eyes.

She came to see me on the advice of a friend. She told me she was coming mostly out of curiosity and that she didn't have any problem, be it physical or psychological. She was very surprised when she became aware of my Italian origins. She told me that she had always been surrounded by Italians in her life, always by coincidence, without a concrete reason. Even her work had her live many years in Italy, even though her family by birth is Catalan. She worked in communications at a high level and her job required her to make many very important decisions every day that could affect the lives of many people, inside and outside her company. Given my past as an executive, that day before the regression we exchanged a few anecdotes about the Italian corporate world. She told me that her family life and her professional life were fine. She had a partner who loved her and two beautiful houses, one a villa in the Veneto and the other in Barcelona. She had no children, she told me, and she did not feel the need for them, nor did she have any particular maternal instinct. When we finished talking I asked her to sit on the chaise longue to proceed with the regression. She fell into a deep trance and began to speak.

"I find myself in a garden, a huge garden. It must be the summer, because the air is warm."

"How are you dressed, and are you a man or a woman?" I asked.

"I'm a woman. I have a large dress, tight at the waist and very wide at the bottom. It reaches my feet. It is white with a pink tinge, made of precious fabric, decorated with ruffles and gold embroidery. I must be quite rich, because this giant park belongs to me. It is the garden of my estate. There is an immense mansion, right behind me. It's so big that my visual field can't see all of it at once, and it is made up of perhaps five or six buildings, one after the other."

"Where is this mansion, do you know?" I asked her.

"I am in Austria."

"How old are you? What is your name?"

"My name is Elisabeth, and I am twenty-two years old."

"What are you doing in the garden?"

"I'm waiting for my husband, who has just now arrived."

"Who is he?" I asked, driven by curiosity.

"His name is Joseph, he is tall and handsome. I am also tall, almost as tall as him. He has blond hair and beautiful blue eyes. He must be an important military man because he is wearing a uniform colored red and blue with details in gold.

I don't think we love each other anymore. Or rather, I know he does not love me anymore. I'm waiting to tell him that I intend to leave the mansion and go live somewhere else for a little while. He no longer consults me for any kind of decision and my opinion seems unimportant to him. I feel useless here."

"Do you have children?" I asked.

"Yes. Two girls and a boy who was born recently. I know the oldest is named Sophia and is five years old. I am sad because I know I cannot take the children with me. I wish I could take them away from here and educate them myself, but he will not let me do it."

"Why? Are you not the mother?"

"Yes. But I hold an important role in the social life of our family and I cannot educate my children myself, it is not allowed."

"What year is it?"

"I don't know. The mid-nineteenth century." She added: "But I know I was born in 1837," as if the information has just come to her.

"I would now like you to go ahead in time to another important event of that life," I then guided her.

"Now I am in another house, a grand villa, but much smaller than the earlier one. It has been a few months. Joseph is not with me, I have only a lady-in-waiting here for company."

"Do you love her?"

"Not particularly, but I am grateful for her because she helps me when I want to get on a horse, she accompanies me during long walks, and she helps me when I need her. She keeps me company, really," she answered, taking for granted the role of a lady-in-waiting at that time.

"Where is this villa?"

"It's in Italy," she said without any hesitation. "Near Venice. I am happy to be here. I love this place. I finally feel free from social pressures and I can devote myself to my own well-being. Even if I am not highly esteemed in these parts, being an Austrian in Italy. I can leave the villa whenever I want, whenever it suits me."

"So are you okay?"

"Yes," she replied, "But I miss my children so badly. I know they are fine, but without them there is a weight in my heart that keeps me from finding peace."

"I understand," I said. "I would like us to go forward again, until the time of your death, Elisabeth's death. I would like you to tell me where you are, how you die, how old you are and if there is someone beside you."

"I'm walking on a bridge, on the banks of a lake. I think I am between forty and fifty years old, certainly not old. I'm waiting for something. Now I see a man is approaching, a stranger, hiding something... A knife. I am struck in the chest before I can scream or run away. I don't feel anything, but now my legs are starting to shake, and I can no longer stand. I fall lifeless."

I guided her permanently away from the life of Elisabeth and we could then understand the teachings the woman had learned in her lifetime. Isabel understood why she had no children in her present life. She was being allowed to recover, to have no responsibility in this regard, none of the suffering that had resulted from being unable to raise her children in her previous life as Elisabeth. She also realized why, in the present, she felt so much satisfaction in her job that required her to make important decisions all the time. It was also in this case a reward, because in her previous life she had been denied the opportunity to make important decisions. Finally, she understood the reason she had so many Italians in her life. It was one final reward for her because she had loved their culture. Elisabeth, because she had been Austrian, was unpopular in Italy in those days for political reasons, and had not gotten the chance to know their customs.

Isabel left my office happy. Not only was she able to relive a past life, but she also had the feeling that her present life was going in the right direction, that her work in Italy was all for a reason, and that her choice not to have children was the right one as well.

But Isabel's story does not end here.

You couldn't imagine my surprise when, as I usually do, in the days following I did some research looking for an Austrian noblewoman who lived in those times, and I realized that Isabel probably had the soul of Elisabeth of Bavaria, Empress of Austria and Queen of Hungary, Bohemia, and Croatia. I remember the heart palpitations that night as I discovered that the details all lined up with what she said, and one after the other—dates, locations, people, descriptions—they all proved accurate. All dead on. I called her immediately and told her what I had discovered. Isabel stood still a moment with her mouth open in a silent stupor. Then she said it was incredible. She called back a few hours later and told me that among the various portraits she saw of Elisabeth, one in particular stirred her emotions. She decided to send it to me. As soon as I received it, I confess I was impressed. I saw it myself, looking into the eyes of the woman in the portrait, the look of the woman who a few days earlier had been in my office. And the surprises did not end there. A few days later she called back again and told me that, despite having never noticed before, a gold pendant she had received from her mother years before and always wore on her neck was made of an old Austrian coin of that era.

Episodes like Isabel's are very rare. Only one of over six hundred regressions, in my case. But this time it wasn't hard to find that it was true. The accuracy of the episodes reported by the woman left no room for interpretation even to my stubborn left hemisphere, the rational part of the brain.

The next regression, that of Oscar, also shows us how the events of our past can somehow directly affect our lives in the present.

Oscar is a young man in his early thirties. He came to me for a concrete problem that affects his daily life, especially his role as a father. He had a two year old baby and was waiting, with his partner, for another child, a girl. Oscar was a man like many others, even in his appearance. During the initial interview I saw no symptoms of a clinical or relational nature except for the one he described to me. He could not show affection for his little firstborn, who was already two years old. He knew it was his son and he loved him, but every time he picked him up he felt a sense of coldness towards the child, which didn't allow him to play with him or demonstrate the outpourings of affection he so desired. Initially I agreed with his diagnosis that this issue was related to the fact that he had lost his father at the tender age of four. He told me that in fact his father was cold and distant to him, and he could not remember a time that his father had demonstrated tenderness to him. However, he confirmed that he had received plenty of affection from his mother and her new partner, her adoptive father, who adored Oscar. The circumstances weren't one hundred percent clear to me. The affection received from his "new" father should have given him the proper emotional development. There was no apparent direct cause-effect relationship to explain his current problem. The reasons for the issue must be sought, once again, in the past.

We decided together to do a regression to his childhood, and I asked Oscar to sit on the couch. Then I proceeded to induce hypnotic relaxation.

"How old are you?" I asked him.

"I am around four years old."

"Where are you?"

"I am in our beach house. It's summer. We came here for vacation. Me, my mother, my father and my oldest sister. She is eight years old."

"Is it day or night?"

"Early afternoon. It's hot. I'm wearing only a bathing suit."

"What room of the house are you in?"

"I'm on the balcony."

"Is there anyone there with you?"

"Yes, my father."

"What are you both doing?"

"He gives me a strong hug, and I smile. He kisses me." While uttering those words, Oscar began to sob loudly. But he was crying tears of deep happiness. "I feel that he really loves me. He is happy to be with me. He tells me I'm his little man. Being in his arms makes me feel safe. I love you, dad!"

But I saw him suddenly take on a terrified look and begin to cry again, this time falling into a deep, endless sadness.

"What happened?" I quickly asked.

He didn't answer, only crying louder and louder. As soon as he calmed down he said "Dad fell to the ground suddenly. My mother, crying and screaming, ran out onto the balcony. She called his name, shaking him, but my father doesn't respond. He's dead. I knew he had a heart attack. My mother told me, but I did not remember that I was the only witness at the exact moment of his death. Now I know he really loved me. I still feel his touch and his kisses, his tight and warm embrace, and the love he felt for me."

Back to a conscious mental state, Oscar had learned that his father loved him, but his mind had erased the memory.

When he was just four years old, his subconscious mind had associated pampering and tenderness with the definitive loss of his father. As a protection mechanism, his own brain had removed that episode from his conscious memory, because it had caused so much pain and would not allow him to continue with his daily life and have any peace as a child.

Our brain, an extremely practical and functional machine, helps us and allows us to face the toughest and most unthinkable situations, precisely calculating the costs and benefits of any action.

Though the cost seemed appropriate for Oscar the baby, they proved incredibly high for Oscar the parent, whose subconscious would not permit him to behave in a way that, erroneously in the eyes of a child, had such a disastrous effect.

Through regression, the man managed to reestablish that precise equilibrium between the conscious and the unconscious mind. Now he knew perfectly that outpourings of emotion, hugs, and displays of affection caused nothing but love.

"I cannot wait to run home and hug my son," Oscar said as we parted ways.

Very similar to Oscar's story is that of Monica, a young woman in her early thirties who came to see me one summer a few years ago. Contrary to previous experience, the reasons for her distress proved, as we shall see, related to events that occurred much further back in time. Monica is a lovely girl, with a proportioned physique. That day she was dressed in a sporty but much sought-after mode, wearing brown jeans with a belt with a large gold buckle, rather expensive-looking high-heel shoes and an elegant beige blouse. A silk scarf from a famous Parisian fashion house, matching her brown hair, completed the look. Her open gaze and radiant smile betrayed an unease that the girl had worn for a long time.

She told me about her unhappy childhood, during which she had to take care of her three younger sisters, taking on the role of her mother, a woman who was absent due to her work, but that's not all. Depressed and negative in spirit, Monica's mother had never shown her honest affection, and was always very critical and would compete with her daughter. Her mother's attitude has produced enormous insecurities in the girl, who projected these decisions today in the present. During the interview she told me that she was not sure to want children, and that this uncertainty had broken up many love stories in her life, making her even more unhappy. She said that she had already played the role of mother with her three sisters and she no longer felt the maternal instinct.

This explanation might make sense in her eyes, but not mine. With experience, I've learned that the majority of the time, especially in the case of women, a lack of parental instinct has roots that go back to past lives, distant memories capable of changing our present destiny.

So I invited her to lie down and proceed with hypnotic relaxation.

"It stinks!" Monica began. "What a nauseating stench. I can hardly breathe. Indeed, her face flushed and her nose wrinkled as if actually sensing some foul-smelling substance. She began to have trouble breathing and I had to use a hypnotic technique to allow her to breathe normally again.

"What is this bad smell?" I then asked her.

"It smells like skins. Animal skins. There are other women here with me. They're tanning and dyeing. What a smell!" and she began to breathe heavily again, forcing me to repeat my technique from earlier.

"It's daytime. It's very hot. And wet. I'm walking in mud. It feels like the desert. My feet are bare. What huge feet!"

"So are you a man?"

"No. I am a woman but I have very big feet," she said, smiling.

"Where are you?"

"I am in Africa, northeast Africa."

"What year is it?"

"921 AD."

"Look at your feet again, please. Do you have dark skin?"

"No. My skin is white."

At first I thought what she was saying didn't make any sense. What would a white-skinned woman be doing in Africa at that time?

"What's your name?" I asked.

"Rania," she answered without hesitation.

"How are you dressed?"

"I'm wearing a light gray dress, made of a strange fabric that looks like leather, long down to the knees, with pockets on the front and a thin belt. I have long red hair, though now it's graying."

"How old are you?" I asked.

"I'm between forty and fifty years old," she replied, uncertain about her exact age.

"Are you married?"

"Yes. To a man much older than me, shorter and uglier. He is truly ugly, with dark skin. But he treats me well. He is dressed much better than me, wearing luxurious clothes."

"Why is that?" I asked.

"He's an official. He collects taxes. He is quite rich."

"But if he is rich, why are you dressed worse and you work at a tannery?" I objected, failing to find any logical sense in her story. A white woman in Africa, in the tenth century, forced by a rich husband, with dark skin, to work in a tannery. It made no sense, at least according to my limited historical knowledge.

"I was sold to him by my own father. I'm not originally from here. I am a slave. I was brought here from Europe, my land."

A white European slave in Africa? This really began to surprise me.

"Who brought you to Africa? Your husband?" I then asked.

"No. Soldiers, men on horseback. I remember they had a red and white flag. I can still remember the sweet gaze of my mother and her long hair, red just like mine. I can also see my father's look as they take me away, he has blue eyes. He never wanted to let me go, but he was forced to."

"Do you have children, you and your husband?"

"No. I cannot have children. But it's better like this. I do not want to have any in these life conditions, although I am grateful that my husband treats me well. I'm happy."

"I understand," I said. She was now sure why she truly lacked a maternal instinct as Monica in her current life. It was not due to her childhood but a memory dating back to her life as a slave in Africa, in Rania's shoes. "I would like you to now go forward in time to the time of your death," I then proposed.

"I am about sixty years old," the girl said. "I am in a bed, in small house made of earth. I have a high fever and blisters all over my body. I am in severe pain."

"Is there someone next to you? Your husband?"

"No. He is not here. Men are not allowed to enter. I'm sick. There are three women with me. One of them is the wife of my husband's brother. We're friends, all the women, and we always help one another. But her husband is younger than the brother. He is also better, and she is not forced to work. There is also an elderly woman who is taking the place of my mother. It is a death ritual."

I asked Monica to leave Rania's body and life so that she could learn the lessons of that existence and permanently get rid of the emotional block that prevented her from being a mother in this life.

Today Monica is a more balanced and peaceful person, especially in regards to her love life. She is finally ready to start a family, willing to give, both to her partner and the children to come, the infinite love that characterizes her essential being.

Later, to my great surprise, I discovered that the woman had been a *Saqaliba*, from the Arabic *Siqlabi*. This term referred to slaves in the medieval Arab world, many of whom were Slavs. Generally taller and with white skin, with white or red hair, they came from Europe. It was exactly what Monica had described. In addition, the name Rania proved to be popular at that time and in those areas.

In our many lives we get the chance to be both parents and children and to learn all facets of the dynamics that characterize these deep relationships. In one life we are children, in another we are parents. We play different roles but always find ourselves as fathers and mothers, sons and daughters, to learn and to demonstrate and share the love that makes us all.

It is important, as parents, to be able to understand that care and demonstrations of affection, be they verbal or physical, are essential for the proper emotional development of our children, as in the case of Oscar. But it is also important, as children, to not blame our parents, but rather understand that they are human beings like us, souls that accompany us during our earthly existence, who we chose in common accord, and they're here to learn lessons just like us. Sometimes when we have children we tend to replicate the mistakes of our parents, and sometimes we behave in the diametric opposite way so as not to resemble them. We should remember that the equilibrium can always be found in the middle.

Personally, I am truly grateful to my parents in this earthly existence for having been close at all times. Without their virtues and their faults, I would not be the person I am. A person who, thanks to their help, I learned to love and respect.

"Nothing has a stronger influence psychologically on their environment and especially their children than the unlived life of the parent."
Carl Gustav Jung

ANIMALS AND SOULS

Animal comes from the Latin word *Anima*, meaning soul. In itself, this simple etymology should answer one of the questions I seem to get most often: Do animals have souls too?

My own experiences confirm the hypothesis that animals do in fact have souls. There are many regressions in which people, in the afterlife, see animals or even perceive themselves as being in the body of an animal, as in the case of Marta, who was a bear in a past life.

Animals serve not only as a spirit guide, as the Native Americans showed for hundreds of years, but they can also be loyal companions in many lives, and even reincarnate several times during the course of our current existence. In fact, it is not uncommon for the soul of Lucky, our beloved dog, to leave us at the end of his life only to return a few years later in the body of our next companion animal. The stories that follow tell us just this, how these pure souls will always accompany us to brighten up our lives and, at times, impart valuable lessons.

When I met Martin, at the reception desk of the center where I do regression therapy, I was struck by his gleaming white smile. The twenty-nine-year-old's perfect teeth made him drastically more attractive. He was tall and his pearly white skin combined with big green eyes gave him an almost angelic presence. When he told me he was from Argentina, I thought that most men of that country are generally attractive, the genetic result of an elaborate mix of cultures.

Martin told me the reason for his visit. He and his fiancee had broken up after a three-year relationship. He felt very sad and wanted to understand if the relationship's sudden end had some karmic nature that would explain things.

I told him first of all that the meaning of the word *karma* is often used incorrectly, in my view. We tend to talk about things like a "karmic debt," mistakenly associating the negativity of the word "debt" with a concept that should be extremely positive. Karma is the totality of the lessons learned from our past actions, allowing us to continue to learn and grow. It's not a matter of "an eye for an eye and a tooth for a tooth," as in the Bible. The purpose of karma isn't to make us suffer but to help us evolve.

He told me that he and his girlfriend had come to Spain together from Argentina a few years ago and they had lived together the whole time since then. After the break-up, Martin had continued to live in the same apartment they had rented. So Kitty, the cat they had had for the past three years and his only current roommate, had stayed to live with him.

He also said that apart from what he had told me already, there was nothing prompting his contacting me, other than perhaps a certain curiosity about the subject of past lives.

I then invited him to lie down on the chaise longue and I induced the hypnotic state.

"No!" Martin suddenly exclaimed, bursting into tears. His face flushed as copious tears began to stream out. He was truly suffering, and even his breathing had become labored.

"What happened? Where are you?" I asked him, intrigued and eager to avoid any unnecessary suffering.

"I'm at my grandmother's house. Mom and dad just died," he said, with the intonation of a small child.

"How old are you?"

"I am six years old," he replied, still speaking like a child. It provokes a strange feeling to hear the voice of a child coming out of a young man.

"What is your name?" I then asked.

"Marie" he said, without any apparent reaction to the idea that he was a little girl in a past life.

"Okay, Marie," I said. "Could you tell me how you're dressed?"

"I'm wearing shoes made of canvas, a strange hard canvas that seems kind of like skin, but it's not. My dress is dark beige and it looks pretty dirty, or stained anyway. I'm wearing a rope belt. I have brown hair, tied in a braid. Grandma did it for me. She is taking care of me now. She is very old, I'm afraid she might die. If she died, I would be all alone. I'm so scared," he added, with the truly worried tone a girl only a few years old might have.

"Could you describe your grandmother? Is she with you?"

"Yes. She's here at home. She has a very humble home. It looks more like a hut, with a wooden roof. It's away from the city, in the middle of the fields. Grandma keeps her white hair in a light scarf tied over her head. The material is very similar to my dress. She's tired because she has to work, but we have no one to help us. She leaves early in the morning. She works first in the fields and then prepares the dough for bread. She taught me how to do it too."

"Can you look her in the eyes, please? If you look into her eyes you will immediately know if her soul is shared by someone you know as Martin in your current life."

"Oh, yes! It's Diana, my younger sister in Martin's life. I realize that I truly love her very much, both as a grandmother in this life and as a sister in my current one, we are united. The difference is that in my current lifetime, I'm the one who has to take care of her."

"What happened to your parents? Why did they die?"

"They got sick. Many people get sick here. Grandmother lives just outside of town and she is not sick, and that's why they brought me here. In the city they are all sick, all dying."

"Where are you?"

"In southern France. It is a small town near Marseille called Arles. I used to live in the city with mom, dad, and my little brother. But all three of them died." Martin burst into tears again. For a few seconds I let him express those emotions.

"What was their illness?" I asked when I saw he had calmed down a bit.

"I don't know. They had a high fever and then they died. They took them away."

"Could we now move to a later time in Marie's life?" I asked.

"Yes. I'm bigger now. I'm twenty-six years old I think."

"What are you wearing?"

"I'm wearing a light brown dress, made of the same canvas from before. Really it's more like rags than a real dress, but it's clean. I'm also wearing a kind of apron on the front and a piece of fabric is holding up my hair."

"What year is it?" I asked.

"It is 1740" Martin replied, with no hesitation.

"Where are you now?"

"I'm walking on a dirt road beside a field."

"Do you live nearby?"

"Yes. I still live in the same house. Grandma died a few years ago. I miss her so much. I was left alone."

"You're not married?"

"No. No one wants to marry me because I have no parents, no family, and therefore no dowry. I have never even fallen in love," Martin added, in a tone that sounded more like resignation than sadness.

"What work do you do?"

"Grandma taught me to make bread, so every day I take the dough I made the day before and I bring it to the city. There is a large communal oven where you can bake bread for a fee. Once it's baked, I take it to the street, in a market where groceries and many other things are sold."

"Can you live on just that?"

"Yes, but I am very poor."

"You don't have friends? Acquaintances?"

"No. I live alone with my dog. I love him very much because he keeps me company and he protects me and my house."

"Could you look at him and describe him for me, please?" I then asked.

"Yes. He is a great big herding dog, completely black... He's Kitty! I am absolutely sure, my black dog has the same soul as Kitty, Martin's cat. He returned in another form in this life. How fantastic!" As Martin said these words, little tears fell down his cheeks. His face took on a serene expression and he seemed to smile. They were tears of joy.

"Would it be alright if we moved to the time of your death now? Marie's death?" I asked the young man, seeing that he was sufficiently calm to address this one last experience.

"Yes, sure," he replied. "It's dark out, about five in the morning, and I find myself at home, in my bed. The house is very small, really just a single room with some basic wooden furniture. My black dog sleeps on the ground next to me. I feel happy, even though I'm all by myself. My life is simple but that's okay."

"How old are you?"

"I'm around forty years old."

"Dying of some disease?" I asked.

"No. I hear footsteps outside, a loud noise," the young man exclaimed. His face mirrored the terror he was feeling as Marie. "They broke down the door. Two soldiers came in. While one stands guard at the door, the other rips off my clothes and forces me to have sex with him," Martin said, after which he stopped talking for a moment.

"What happened?" I asked, to understand this sudden silence in such a dramatic moment.

"I can't talk. He's keeping my mouth shut with one hand while abusing my body. But it's better this way. If I cried out, my dog would come out from behind the cabinet where he's hidden and they would kill him. I hope it ends quickly and they go away without harming him," the young man said, and went on. "Now the first soldier has left and the second one is coming in. He's abusing me too. I silently cry hoping that the violence will end soon. Oh no! No!" Martin screamed in terror.

"What's happening now?"

"He pulled out a sword and has impaled me between the legs. As a final show of disregard for me. I feel the pain, strong and hollow. And I cry out desperately. I see the dog jump on his neck, bite him, and blood spews out from the soldier's jugular. But now the first soldier comes back in and kills my poor dog, cutting cleanly through his head with a sword. The pain is gone. I feel that I have no strength left and life has fled my body. But I'm serene. Thanks to my little buddy, my companion in so many moments of solitude, who did not hesitate to give his life to protect me."

"Okay," I then said, and guided us along: "Now leave Marie's body and view the scene from above, please. What have you learned from that life?"

"I learned the value of humility and simplicity," Martin said. Effectively, by what he had told me during the interview, and despite his handsome looks, he seemed to be a truly humble person.

"Anything else?"

"Yes. That life exists in all forms and must be respected. That animals are beings of light and love, just like us. Their souls are pure. I really loved my dog and he took care of me until the end."

"I would like you to leave Marie's life for good now, if that's okay for you." I told the young man.

"I'm going up higher and higher. I am among the clouds in the sky. Climbing even higher now. The clouds are gone, as is the sky. There is only an incredibly strong white light, but it is good. It's as if I could float. I feel weightless and completely at peace. I feel a sensation of incredible lightness. A serenity I've never felt before. A truly deep love." His body relaxed completely, as well as the expression on his face.

"Have you ever felt a feeling of love so strong as this in your life?" I asked Martin in that moment.

"Only once, in the arms of my mother when I was born," he said, and began to cry tears of joy.

Like all of us, the only time the young man had actually felt such a strong feeling of love was immediately after his birth.

When we are born into this life, for only a few moments we are still able to experience, physically, that feeling of infinite love which is our true essence. Before we are reborn in the human dimension we are spiritual beings, consisting of such a powerful light and love, as Martin just described, which now, thanks to the experience of regression, we are able to experience again.

"I get to meet my black dog," the young man said happily, with his eyes closed but his expression showing the joy he was feeling. "He is floating in the clouds, and approaching me. He licks my hand. As he's licking my hand, words appear in my mind as if he is actually saying them: *We'll always be together.* I am happy. I know we will be together again. I know. He's Kitty. My cat. And he's returned to my life to be with me again. Now Kitty always sleeps in bed with me. She wakes me up every morning with outpourings of love."

Martin, thanks to the regression, understood that his karma, which he mistakenly thought of as a debt he would have to pay back, had nothing to do with his romantic ups and downs and the relationship that had just ended. Marie's existence showed the purity of his soul and the positive lessons that had been learned in the shoes of a French peasant. He had experienced the hard way how love has no form or gender and that all of us, beings of the universe, are made in the same fashion.

Pamela, the star of the next story, also showed the connection that binds us, as human beings, to the animal world.

She was a small woman with a perfectly composed body, a little over thirty years old. It was a very hot that summer afternoon and she was dressed lightly of course. Although she was a sweet and graceful person, it seemed she hadn't put much care into getting ready that day. Her shirt was on backwards, with a large white label showing at the collar. Her long blond hair was only combed at the fringe, and her eye makeup wasn't done properly. After talking for a few minutes, I realized that those details were not out of place due to her carelessness, but because she really didn't have the time. She told me that she was married and working full-time. She said she rarely saw her husband anymore and never got to talk to him. According to her, it wasn't a problem because they had never truly been in love. They met a few years ago. He was older, and he found her as the answer to his mid-life crisis. She, young and orphaned, found in him the father figure she so dearly missed. So far, her story was similar to many other women.

IT'S NEVER THE END

In addition to her commitments at work and in the home, Pamela also took great satisfaction in running an animal shelter. She provided daily care for dozens of abandoned dogs and cats, offering them love and a home. Unfortunately, over the years this commitment had created tensions in her family life. She told me that she had had many partners in her life but have never truly felt loved. She came to find out if this lack of love had roots far back in another time. She privately felt that feeling loved was important and something that she, like everyone else, was entitled to. She didn't understand the reason for this void in her life and it made her feel different from other people. That feeling kept her from living a happy and fulfilling life.

Before getting started with the regression, that day I decided to read Pamela a few sentences I had bookmarked just a few weeks before after reading a review of one of the Dalai Lama's books:

"It is necessary to reflect on the essential nature of relationships. This is the starting point. Often it comes from a selfish nature, and therefore causes much friction... In a couple, the relationship is often based more on attachment than on true love. It is built according to the projections of the two partners who, starting from their desires and expectations, exert a certain influence on each other and they love to be loved. For example, romantic love. The powerful desire and arousal emphasize the positive qualities of the partner and, conversely, exaggerate their defects when attitude begins to change or when the partner stops corresponding to the image constructed of them... When our projections change, the at-

tachment decreases because, in this case, love is based not on the desire to make one another happy but on a selfish need that has prevailed over reason."

I waited a few seconds, so that she could fully understand the meaning, and then I asked her to sit on the couch and I began by inducing the trance. She reached the trance in just a few seconds, which just goes to show how the same state of consciousness can be difficult for some to achieve and incredibly easy for others.

"I'm walking through the forest," the woman began.

"Look at your feet, please, and tell me about them," I asked her.

"They are a woman's feet. I'm barefoot. My skin is not dark, but rather a bit tanned."

"How are you dressed?"

"Everything I'm wearing was once living. I also have a necklace made of animal teeth. I have long black hair. It's curly and tied back in a bun behind my head with green stones. There are amulets on my arms made of animal teeth and bits of tortoise shell."

"How do you feel?"

"I feel at ease. It's so beautiful. There are lots of plants with leaves of all shapes and sizes. I seem to know them all. They're important to us. Some of the plants we eat, others treat diseases. They are many different shades of green. I don't think I have ever seen so many."

"I see," I said.

What Pamela referred to made sense. The human eye is, in fact, more sensitive to frequencies of green light, and is able to perceive countless shades of it. This peculiarity is due to the fact that the first forms of life that appeared anywhere on Earth were plants, which represent an important source of food, the basis of our food chain. This omnipresence of green requires our visual organ to distinguish each particular shade to have the best chance of survival, whether in hunting or in the selection of food. Just what Pamela was experiencing.

"How old are you?" I then asked her.

"Twenty-one."

"Is it day or night?"

"It's starting to get dark. I am collecting firewood for the night, for the fire. It protects us from the animals."

"Where are you?"

"In America, I think Mexico."

"What year is it?"

"966." "Are you married?"

"Yes. My husband is the most important person in the tribe. Sort of a leader. He's a warrior. I still remember when we got married. He chose me from over twenty-five suitors because I was the most beautiful. He loves me so much, and he respects me. I love him too, and it was a great honor for me to be chosen. As a symbol of his love, he gave me necklaces and other ornaments that I carry to this day."

"What is he like?"

"He's a bit taller than me. He has a tanned complexion, long black hair like me, and he wears an ornament made of parrot feathers."

"Do you have children?"

"Yes, we have three children. We also had a fourth who died a few years ago. He never returned from the forest. Perhaps he got lost or was killed during the hunt."

"Are you sad about this?"

"No. For us it's absolutely normal. Animals and nature give us life, but we give them life as well. It's the order of things. I have no problems with this."

"Okay," I said, and led her to the time at the end of that existence.

"A puma assaulted me. He was waiting for me on a tree. He heard me coming. He leapt at me and I came crashing to the ground. I'm already dead. It all happened very quickly, didn't even hurt."

"How old were you?"

"Thirty-four," Pamela responded. Her face took on an expression of bliss.

"Are you out of her body?" I asked, seeing that beautiful expression.

"Yes. I learned a lot from this life. Firstly, the importance of animals and nature. We did not think we were better than them. We lived in harmony with the animals. They were a great danger but also our livelihood, and we were their livelihood. I felt a great respect for them. Being killed by a puma was almost considered a privilege. It is the king of the forest, and I was the wife of a king. There was balance," she continued, "and man is no better than the animals. We have to respect them and treat them as we do our fellow men. We can learn a lot from them. They are our masters. And so is nature. We must respect them and love them as we do ourselves. We are made of the same energy as the plants and the animals. They are like us. We are the same."

I listened carefully. Pamela was reminding me of something precious. I thought that too often we pursue our frenetic technological life, with our cynical, blind egos, and we forget the true nature of the animals.

In subsequent sessions, Pamela found that in her many past lives, she had experienced more than one romantic love, hardly denied the feeling of love at all. She was desired, loved, and respected in ancient Rome, in Mongolia more than a thousand years earlier, in 19th century America, in medieval France, and even as the wife of a Viking. On more than one occasion, she had gotten to learn the lessons of romantic love, how to live with passion and live life as a couple. In her current existence she was instead being given the opportunity to learn other lessons, such as to respect animals, like her beloved dogs and cats. They provide their own rewards through the purity of their love, that same selfless love of the black dog in Martin's story, who did not hesitate to give his life away to save his lady in distress. Today Pamela is surrounded by a form of love that is different from romance, but is no less strong or important.

Animals are our faithful companions in life and also teachers from whom we can learn great lessons. They can stay by our side, returning in more than one existence, and even accompany us in various forms during the course of the same life.

They know a form of love that's different from human love. What they feel is pure, unfiltered by the ego, and comes directly from their essence, their soul. And they don't ask anything in return.

"Many primitives assume that a man has a 'bush soul' as well as his own, and that this bush soul is incarnate in a wild animal or a tree, with which the human individual has some kind of psychic identity.... If the bush soul is

that of an animal, the animal itself is considered as some sort of brother to the man."
Carl Gustav Jung

SOUL MATES

Do soul mates really exist?

Judging by the hundreds of regressions I have assisted with, I would say yes. But it depends on how we define "soul mate." The common idea of a soul mate is someone who should be your true partner, the object of your greatest love in this life. Perhaps this imaginary soul mate would even give you a whole and happy life. *"And they lived happily ever after,"* as we hear in fairy tales when we're children. But is it always like this?

Absolutely not. Our celestial family, the group of souls with whom we travel through many lives in order to learn lessons, is very large. Imagine a big, crowded lecture hall big enough to accommodate every student who would sign up for the course. One day we may end up sitting next to one person, then the next day we might sit next to a different person, who was previously sitting somewhere else dozens of seats away. Our souls move around the same way. In one life we can end up next to a person, a soul mate or even more than one soul mate, whereas in another life our life companions change entirely. As in that lecture hall, nothing prevents us from sitting next to the same person again for several days in a row either. The same happens during our many lifetimes. We repeatedly encounter the same soul, perhaps in a loved one, or a soul mate, you might say.

So it is not the case that our soul mate must necessarily be our actual partner in our current life. He or she can return to live with us as our best friend, our mother, a teacher or a work colleague. In any case, they leave an indelible imprint on our life. They help us in the learning process. They make for an exceptional teacher. But sometimes the lessons can be difficult to understand, so don't be too angry if sometimes they make us suffer.

It seems appropriate here to quote an interesting definition of soul mate, that of Elizabeth Gilbert in her book *"Eat, Pray, Love"*:

"People think a soul mate is your perfect fit, and that's what everyone wants. But a true soul mate is a mirror, the person who shows you everything that is holding you back, the person who brings you to your own attention so you can change your life. A true soul mate is probably the most important person you'll ever meet, because they tear down your walls and smack you awake."

We can often feel unlucky and think we haven't yet found love, or that the latest stage of our life has been a disaster. And then we begin to search again for our soul mate, without realizing that our soul mate may well have been the person we just left. And his or her role as the soul mate in our life was simply terminated.

We can only truly understand who was our soul mate afterwards, when we can assess the great changes that person introduced into our lives.

Furthermore, a soul mate doesn't even have to be found in someone's body. Just because it's not physically right next to us in this life doesn't mean he or she isn't next to us as a soul. We can meet them in this current life, if we haven't already, or in other lives. But a soul mate can accompany us every day independent of their physical condition. Soul mates never leave us.

In other existences, however, our earthly reality is more like our collective fairytale imagination, and that's easier to understand when we really are in the presence of our soul mate. In these lives, we can just look deep into their eyes and know in our heart that we have been with them forever.

This is the case with Veronica, our next story's protagonist. Veronica showed up at my office on a midsummer day. She was a twenty-three-year-old girl, not too tall or too short, with long straight reddish hair that fell to the middle of her back. She had large brown eyes, straight facial features. Anyone would have said she was a pretty girl, even though she wasn't wearing makeup. She wore ripped jeans and a burgundy tank top that left her back completely bare. Her body was slender but muscular, a lovely figure.

"What do you do for work?" I asked, curious, seeing her athletic body.

"I'm a ballerina," Veronica said, confirming my hypothesis. "I really like my job. It's a passion for me more than anything. I've done it since childhood. I've won big competitions and it has made me happy. I've also started to teach at my dancing school." The girl's eyes sparkled with joy as she told me about her profession.

"What's a girl of your age doing here?" I then asked.

I always ask about the younger people who come to see me, because most people don't see the need to search for spirituality until their older years.

"Mostly curiosity," she said. "But I'm also very afraid of death. I don't have a reason to be, but thinking about it terrifies me."

"Don't worry, I understand. Surely we can do something about that," I answered.

I knew that losing one's fear of death was one of the most common benefits of regression. I myself had lost that fear after my own first regression.

Despite her beauty, the girl had yet to have much luck in love. She had had brief relationships but they never developed into anything important.

She had no reason to worry just yet, given her young age, but she told me that she wanted to find her soul mate.

"If you have no other questions, shall we proceed with the regression?" I said.

"Yes, but I have just one more question," the girl said. "How do you decide which life to take me to? I imagine I've probably lived a good many. How do you choose the right one? Why one and not the other?" she asked.

"It's simple," I said. "It's not for me to decide. It's your own soul that chooses which life to show. I'm just a vessel. I apply a hypnotic technique that allows you to receive the information that your soul wants you to know. Normally, I can tell you from experience, the first life we are shown is the one that's most important to us at that time. The one that has the most impact on our present life. One where the memories of those events can help to improve our present. The soul is wise and knows what life to prioritize and show us before another. Let's leave it to the soul, how about that?" I joked, and invited Veronica to lie down and begin the session.

"I am a woman," she began.

"Are you inside a building or outdoors? Is it day or night?" I asked immediately, setting our focus.

"I'm in a room, in a mansion. The room is big and bright."

"Do you live there?"

"Yes. I live here. It's my bedroom. There is a large four-poster bed here with carved wooden columns. The home is very elegant."

"What's your name?"

"Rose" Veronica responded without hesitation.

"How old are you?"

"I'm twenty-three years old, just like the present."

"Where are you?"

"I'm in the north of France."

"What year is it?"

"1764."

"How are you dressed?"

"I'm wearing a white dress. It's embroidered, made of a precious fabric. The neckline is large and rectangular, with ruffles. The sleeves come to my forearms and are tastefully decorated. I have very fair skin, it looks like white milk. I'm sitting in front of a wooden dressing table with a mirror and getting ready. I can see myself. I'm young and beautiful. I have my hair tied behind my head. My hair is bulky and looks white, almost purplish... How weird! Oh of course, it's a wig."

"Is there anything else that catches your attention?" I asked, seeing that her facial expression changed.

"Yes. I'm wearing a big silver ring with a precious oval green stone in it. I think it's an engagement ring."

"Are there any other people around you?"

"My governess is in the room, helping me to prepare. My father and mother are in other rooms in the house."

"Could you describe them to me?"

"Yes. My mother is slimmer and shorter than me. Her hair is weird like mine, but her wig is even more massive than mine, with huge curls on the side of her head. My father wears a smaller white wig. He's wearing several layers of different outfits, with a very elaborate green jacket on top."

"You seem to be dressed very elegantly. You told me you're preparing. Where are you going?"

"I'm getting married!" Veronica exclaimed, suddenly, with excitement. "It's my wedding day."

"What is your future husband like?"

"He's tall and so, so handsome. His name is Alexandre. He has long brown hair, but today he's going to wear a wig as well. He is smartly dressed with a strange, straight, high collar. I can see his beautiful green eyes. I love him so much and I know he loves me back. I'm so happy!" she said, starting to cry from the joy and emotion, as if she really were getting married.

"What's happening now?" I asked, after giving her a few minutes to fully enjoy her profound happiness.

"He tells me he loves me more than anything in the world and he's giving me the wedding ring. It's a brilliant stone, smaller than the green one but much more precious, mounted on a ring. It's really amazing. I look at my mother and see she's crying from all the emotion," Veronica then said, herself starting to cry.

I waited a few minutes then asked if she wanted to explore a later moment in Rose's existence. She agreed.

"Where are you now? How old are you?"

"I'm very sick. I have a fever. I'm pale, I'm sweating and I feel cold at the same time," the girl said.

Seeing that she was actually starting to sweat, even there in my office, I had to quickly use hypnotic suggestion to limit her uncomfortable feelings and proceed with the regression.

"How do you feel now?" I asked her.

"I'm not cold anymore. Physically I feel fine, but I know I still have a fever. I'm in a carriage. They're bringing me to the hospital. My husband and mother are with me."

"How old are you?" I asked, understanding, given the presence of her mother, that she likely was dying young.

"I'm twenty-seven years old. I'm dying of tuberculosis."

"Okay. Leave Rose's life and body then. What have you learned? What were the lessons of that life?"

"It was a short but intense life. I was very lucky. Very happy. I got to experience earthly love. My husband loved me so much and I loved him. Now I know he is my soul mate. I'm continuing to get information from that life, and he's telling me not to be afraid for our love because we will meet again. I know I will see him again. I'm absolutely certain. I know he'll never leave me and that we'll continue to live together, forever."

Veronica wasn't mistaken that day. As usual, the information she received from the regression proved accurate. A couple of months later she came back to see me and told me she had met a young man who became her boyfriend after a couple of weeks. They were very much in love with one another. They had met randomly, as the boy lived more than five hundred kilometers away from her. It had been love at first sight. They only had to look into each other's eyes to know. They were already talking about moving in together. Veronica had told me clearly that, when she looked into her boyfriend's eyes, she saw the soul of Alexandre, Rose's beloved husband. She had found her soul mate and they were back together, and happy.

But that wasn't the last surprise. Veronica and her new boyfriend did in fact move in together. After a few months of living together she told him about her experience during the regression and asked him to consider trying out the technique as well. In fact, the girl asked him to do a regression using my audio recording. The audio track was uploaded on YouTube and Vimeo the year prior. The recording was from a group regression I had done with almost two hundred participants during a seminar. He was initially skeptical, but one day he gave in and conceded to his beloved's desires.

The girl told me that on that occasion she saw herself as Betsy, a young woman in Seattle, USA in 1962, while she was out bowling with a group of friends. She saw a young man bowling named Frank, and she immediately recognized her boyfriend's soul in him. She was very much in love with him, even in Betsy's life, and he reciprocated. Despite the fact they were doing the regression with just a recording rather than me in the flesh, she even saw the time of Betsy's death, which occurred due to a car accident. Frank, the bowler, her lover, was driving a high speed sports car, racing with another driver and driving in the opposite lane. She was sitting in the passenger seat. He died instantly when they collided with another vehicle going the opposite direction. She felt her soul leave Betsy's body and saw Frank's bloody head on the steering wheel. She also told me that while leaving Betsy's body, her only desire was to come back and see her love again. He really is her soul mate, I supposed.

At the end of the recording, Veronica anxiously asked her boyfriend what he had seen. And you cannot imagine my surprise when she told me that he saw the Black Mountains, in Canada, only a few hours by car from Seattle. He told her he was in a forest with huge, tall trees, in a cold and wild place. He didn't live there, but he had gone there in search of gold, a way for him to earn good money. His friends called him *Racer* because of his passion for fast cars. He also told her that during his regression, after he died he felt he had reached a place filled with light. There, a celestial guide told him not to worry because he hadn't truly lost his love. He and Betsy would be together forever.

The story of Veronica and her boyfriend is really extraordinary, soul mates who live together in this life lived together more than fifty years before.

Just a few months after her first regression, the girl's life had truly changed. Now she not only knew she had a soul mate, but she had him beside her every day. That same man who had always loved her, in the role of Alexandre in eighteenth-century France and as Frank in sixties America, had returned to her side to take care of her again.

Christian, the protagonist of our next story, also had an experience that shows us love has no limits in scope or duration.

Christian came to me on a winter afternoon a few years ago. He showed up muddy and bedraggled, as I remember that day it had rained enough to force the authorities to close a few flooded metro stations. He had short dark hair, and plenty of it for a forty-eight-year-old man. His eyes were big and brown, and his nose looked distinguished. From his features and the way he flaunted them, it was clear that he must have been handsome as a young man. He wore a sports shirt and a pair of jeans which were wet up to his knees. I immediately turned on the room's heater and, before we could start, I waited for his pants to dry a little while I asked him the reason for his visit. He told me he was mostly driven by curiosity, but also because despite not being a young man anymore, he still hadn't found his true love. He had married early and had two daughters, but a managerial career had kept him away from them. Although he loved his wife, they ended up separated after eighteen years of living together. The separation had been followed by a stable relationship with a new partner that lasted eight years, but that was over now too. I asked him if he had loved, and still did love, one or both of the women. He said yes, that he was very fond of his wife and his former partner, but he had the distinct feeling that he had never felt a very deep love for either one of them.

I asked him a few questions to gauge his mental state and satisfy myself that this feeling of a lack of love wasn't due to some psychological or personality issue that would lead me to suggest a psychiatrist or clinical psychologist. Christian, however, seemed to be perfectly coherent, at least in my eyes.

Meanwhile, I noticed his pants had dried and suggested we start the regression. After the hypnotic induction, Christian spontaneously began to speak.

"I'm in the middle of a small village. It is cloudy and quite cold. There are many people here and there is a well in the center of the square. The buildings are made of stone, gray as the sky. There is a loud, strange music. We're all dancing. It's a big party."

"How are you dressed?" I asked.

"I'm wearing a green skirt that ends at my knees," the man replied. "It's dark green, made of a very heavy fabric that feels like felt. But I'm not a woman! My legs are hairy and muscular. I'm a man in a skirt!" He began to giggle, unable to make sense of it.

"What else are you wearing?"

"Heavy gray socks made of wool. And dark brown men's shoes covered in mud. I'm wearing a kind of vest, also very heavy, that feels like leather. I have long red hair and a big bushy beard. My complexion is ruddy, but maybe just because I'm drunk right now. I'm dancing with my arms around the woman I love. It's a pretty funny dance, we're kind of hopping around."

"What's she like? Could you describe her for me?"

"Yes. She's really beautiful. She has reddish hair, long and beautiful locks of it. She has delicate features and a white complexion, with her cheeks reddened from our dancing, and blue eyes. I'm very attracted to her. I love her with all I've got. I've never loved anyone so much." Tears began to fall from his closed eyes.

"You've never felt anything like this in your current life?" I asked Christian.

"No. Never. My love for her pervades my whole body. While we dance and I look in her eyes, it's like we're melting together."

"What's her name?"

"Laura."

"And what's your name?"

"Charles."

"Where are you, geographically speaking?"

"We're in Scotland."

"What year is it?"

"1446."

"How do you feel?"

"I'm so happy. I know that Laura and I are getting married. We are engaged and we've promised one another our eternal love. Soon I'll have to leave for a battle. There are wars between the various villages. But as soon as I get back, we'll be married. We love each other so much."

"Would you mind if we moved forward to a later time in Charles' life, to see what happens?" I asked Christian.

"I'm making love with Laura," the man said a few minutes later. His face was red and his facial expressions were changing to show the passion he was feeling in the moment. "I've never made love like this. I hold her in my arms and I feel a great pleasure, infinite love. As if the two of us are one body."

I let him fully enjoy the moment. When at last his body and face relaxed, I got back to the questions.

"What's happening now?"

"I'm at the battle, in an immense field. The sky is cloudy and it's very cold. There are many of us, proceeding forward in rank and file. My best friend is right next to me. He also has a beard and red hair. We look a lot alike. We've known each other since childhood, always great friends, the same age growing up in the same village. I trust him. He's like a brother."

"Could you look deeply into his eyes, please?" I asked. "Tell me if his soul belongs to someone you know in your life as Christian today."

"Yes. He's my uncle. My father's brother. We don't have a great relationship in this life. I can't stand him. I never understood why, but it's all clear to me now."

"What do you mean?"

"We are preparing for the assault and running towards the enemy. We begin to fight. I kill several people then I get injured, my arm's hurt. Suddenly I feel a sword stab me from behind in the right flank. I turn around and I discover, to my horror, that my best friend is the murderer. I fall to the ground in pain and my eyes fix on him as he walks away as if nothing had happened, continuing to fight. Little by little, the pain disappears. I'm dying. I leave my body and feel a wonderful sense of peace and well-being, which is mixed with anger and disbelief at my friend's absurd, baseless betrayal. While abandoning the body of Charles, I understand what will happen after the battle. My best friend will come back and marry Laura, my beloved. His feigned sorrow for my death unites them, making sure she loves him. I feel an immense pain and frustration. I continue to climb higher and higher into the sky. Now the clouds disappear and are replaced with a bright, clear light. Peace and love take over. Laura is next to me, or even better, her soul. Wordlessly, she tells me that I need not worry, that our love is eternal and will never end, and we'll be together in another life. She whispers, be calm and don't hurry. She won't return in this life, and Christian won't get a chance to see her again, but I must wait for a future, happy life. We will be back together, and she'll never leave again."

I brought the man back to a normal state of consciousness and he didn't speak for several minutes. He had surprise written on his face. Later, he confirmed that he was very happy because he finally understood what it was like to feel a deep, profound love. He, too, had a soul mate and felt the strong, clear presence of Laura at his side at all times. He felt her love and he reciprocated. He was a truly complete man now. He knew that she would continue to love him in another dimension and that he only had to be patient. She would be back with him in another life.

A soul mate is next to us at all times, even if not in a physical form, as in the case of Christian—Charles in his past life—and Laura, though it may seem incredible.

It's difficult to accept that Christian will never even know the person he most deeply loves in this life. But they shared a past life, and they'll share a future one. Their souls have actually never left one another. They are soul mates who will always travel together, through time and space. Although physically separated, Charles and Laura are forever united by the strongest force there is, love.

The next story shows us how you can return to love after a very long time, as did Marta, the same girl who saw herself as a bear in the forest. She came to see me for the third time from Italy, and I felt an immense gratitude towards her for having done so. Meeting her is always a pleasure, as her energy can illuminate any person or place. With her, we've already dealt with and resolved several issues, thanks to numerous regressions. And what we found out that day did nothing but confirm what she already knew in her heart.

After saying hello and doing a little small talk, I asked her to sit on the chaise longue and close her eyes. I then proceeded to induce a deep state of hypnotic relaxation. It turned out to be pretty simple, not only due to her natural disposition, but also because achieving a trance can take practice. And with Marta, we had done this enough before to make it easy.

"I'm wearing brown leather sandals. The soil around me is dark," the girl began.

"Are you a man or a woman?"

"I'm a man. My skin is dark. I'm wearing a bright coat made of natural fibers. It looks very old. I'm Egyptian."

"What's your name?"

"Eliyah."

"How old are you?"

"I'm twenty-eight years old."

"Where are you?"

"I'm in Mesopotamia."

"What year is it?"

"321 A.D."

"What are you doing?"

"I'm running away. They're chasing me."

"Who's chasing you?"

"The others. I defected. I should have gone with them but I don't believe in the war. It's stupid and doesn't solve anything. It brings only destruction and suffering. We think we are different but we aren't. We are all the same.

I want to stay at home with my wife. I love her so much. We have two children and are expecting a third."

"Okay. I would now like to go to an important moment in Eliyah's life," I told Marta.

"I'm at home," she said. "It's a stone hut with a thatched roof. I'm looking at my wife as she gives birth. I'm so happy to be here with her. I feel very proud to be a father again. She is twenty-six years old, two years younger than me. She's so beautiful and I love her so, so much."

"Could you look into her eyes for me please?"

"Yes. I can see her eyes clearer and clearer. A slightly green shade of blue. She doesn't have bright eyes, but I see in her eyes a light that I've only ever seen in my current partner. Her eyes are the same, have the same soul. From the day I met him, in this present life, I knew we had already met when I looked in his eyes. I always knew he was a soul mate. And now at least I have proof."

"Was your child born?"

"Yes. He's a boy. And the others are boys too."

"Could we now proceed to later on in Eliyah's life?" I then asked Marta. She agreed.

"It's the moment of my death. I'm fighting. In the end I had no choice. I had to go to war. It's only been a year, so I'm twenty-nine. For that reason I didn't want to leave, because I knew I would die and have to leave my loved ones. I'm hit with a spear that pierces me between the heart and the shoulder. It's a bad wound, and I fall to the ground."

"Now leave the life of Eliyah," I told her, seeing she was suffering.

"I feel free and light now. I'm floating above the scene, seeing my body lying on the ground. And I continue to go up, up, further up. I feel calm because I know I will see my beloved wife, and we'll meet again, as almost two thousand years later we're still together, forever united. In truth, it's like we never left one another. Now I sense a presence next to me. I think it's some kind of master or celestial guide. I ask him what his name is, and he only replies that during a previous earthly existence they called him *"The King."* He came to remind me that war is futile because we are all united, all perfect and wonderful beings."

"And he has a message for you, too," Marta added, to my surprise.

"What?" I asked, feeling both stupefied and honored.

"It will be possible to explain how the universe works only when you come to understand time." *The King* said.

AKNOWLEDGEMENTS

My deepest love and gratitude go to Dr. Brian Weiss and his wife Carole. Their knowledge and dedication to this subject not only changed my life but also allowed me to change the lives of many other people.

Thank you Valentina Camerini and Donica Raco Sapiano for your great help in making this book more enjoyable and easy to read.

I am also thankful to my loving family, my parents, my brother Ennio Valerio and his wife Giuliana, my niece Elena and my special aunts.

I extend my gratitude to Patrizia Perricone, Emanuela Bertozzini, Bel Cotes, Fabrizio Gelli who helped me become a better person and to Barbara Barsi, Micaela Picozzi, Silvia Zomparelli, Giorgio Gandolfo for their moral support.

Finally, I am especially grateful to all the wonderful people whose stories are described in this book.

ABOUT THE AUTHOR

Alex B. Raco, Specialist in Anxiety and Mood Disorders, earned his Diploma at the University of León in Spain. His postgraduate education includes a Diploma in Clinical Psychopathology from the University of Barcelona, a Diploma in Ericksonian Hypnosis from the University of Valencia and professional training in Clinical Hypnosis at the Autonomous University of Madrid. He also underwent a four-year jungian psychoanalysis treatment.

He attended the professional Past Life Regression Therapy training with Dr. Brian Weiss at the Omega Institute for Holistic Studies in Rhinebeck, New York.

M.B.A. from Bocconi University of Milan, and graduate from The American University of Rome, before dedicating himself to Past Life Regressions he worked as an executive for several multinational companies.

Printed in Great Britain
by Amazon